Life Form™

User's Guide

fitnesoft

Version 1.00.05
©Fewer Tiers, Inc. 1997
All Rights Reserved.
Printed in U.S.A.

Fitnesoft, Inc. •11 East 200 North • Orem, UT • 84057
Support: Telephone (801)221-7708 • Fax: (801)221-7707

SOFTWARE LICENSE AGREEMENT

GRANT OF RIGHTS

Fitnesoft, Inc. (Fitnesoft) grants the right to use the software product Life Form (Software) in accordance with the terms and conditions listed in this Agreement. If the Software is purchased for an individual, then that individual may install and use the Software on any computer which is owned or used by that individual. Members of that individual's immediate family may also use the software on any computer owned or used by that individual.

 If the Software is purchased for a school, then the school may install and use the Software on any or all computers in one room at the school. The room may be a classroom, a computer lab, or an office.

If the Software is purchased for an entity other than an individual or school, such as a business or a government agency, then that entity may install and use the Software on one computer at a time.

The making of copies of the Software is allowed in support of the authorized use of the Software, including backup and archival purposes.

RESTRICTIONS

The making of copies of the Software for purposes other than those listed in this Agreement is prohibited. Renting or leasing the Software without the written permission of Fitnesoft, Inc. is prohibited. Decompilation, disassembly, reverse engineering, copying, or creating a derivative work of the Software are also prohibited.

LIMITED WARRANTY/LIMITATION OF LIABILITY

This Software is licensed AS IS. If for any reason you are dissatisfied with the Software, return the product package with proof of purchase, to your dealer within 90 days of purchase for a full refund. If your dealer will not grant you a refund, return the product package with proof of purchase to Fitnesoft, Inc. within 90 days of purchase for a full refund. If any materials or media in this package are defective, return them to Fitnesoft, Inc. within 90 days of the date of purchase, and they will be replaced at no charge.

THESE WARRANTIES ARE IN LIEU OF ANY OTHER WARRANTIES, EXPRESS OR IMPLIED, INCLUDING THE IMPLIED WARRANTIES OF MERCHANTABILITY AND FITNESS FOR A PARTICULAR PURPOSE. IN NO EVENT WILL FITNESOFT BE LIABLE TO YOU FOR DAMAGES, INCLUDING ANY LOST PROFITS, LOST SAVINGS, OR OTHER INCIDENTAL OR CONSEQUENTIAL DAMAGES ARISING OUT OF YOUR USE OR INABILITY TO USE THE SOFTWARE, EVEN IF FITNESOFT OR AN AUTHORIZED FITNESOFT REPRESENTATIVE HAS BEEN ADVISED OF THE POSSIBILITY OF SUCH DAMAGES.

Some jurisdictions do not allow excluding or limiting implied warranties of limiting liability for incidental or consequential damages, and some jurisdictions have special statutory consumer protection provisions that may supersede this limitation. As a result, this limitation of liability may not apply to you if prohibited by the laws of your jurisdiction.

CUSTOMER SUPPORT

Fitnesoft will attempt to answer your technical support requests concerning the Software, however, this service is offered on a reasonable efforts basis only, and Fitnesoft may not be able to resolve every support request. Support policies may change from time to time without notice.

GENERAL

If any provision of this Agreement is found to be unlawful, void or unenforceable, then that provision shall be severed from this Agreement and will not affect the validity and enforceability of any of the remaining provisions. This Agreement shall be governed by the laws of the State of Utah.

ANY QUESTIONS?

If you have any questions concerning the terms of this Agreement, please write or call Fitnesoft at 11 East 200 North, Suite 204, Orem, Utah 84057, 801/221-7707 (Fax), 801/221-7708 (Customer Service), info@fitnesoft.com, or support@fitnesoft.com.

CodeBase++ 5 DLL Sub-License Agreement

This legal document is an agreement between you, the CodeBase++ 5DLL SUB-LICENSEE, and the CodeBase++ 5 LICENSEE (hereinafter referred to as the "Agreement").

You are not being "sold" any Sequiter Software Inc. software. Instead, you are being granted the right to use Sequiter Software Inc. software through this license agreement. Sequiter Software Inc. retains all ownership of its software including all copies of its software.

1.   **Definitions**

1.1 Software: This is the Sequiter Software Inc. computer programs contained in this Code Base++ 5 software package or any computer programs containing parts of the computer programs in this package. These programs could be represented in any form including print, electronic source code, compiled object modules, a library file, a dynamic link library, an executable program, or any other form.

1.2 Executable Software: This is a binary form of the Software which can be executed directly by a computer.

1.3 Distributable Software: This is any Executable Software except for the CodeReporter executable program.

1.4 Licensed Software Environment: Licensed Software Environments consist of the DOS, Microsoft Windows and OS/2 operating systems.

1.5 DLL Software: This is a dynamic link library form of the Software which is executed indirectly. It includes Microsoft Windows and OS/2 dynamic link library forms of the Software. For the purpose of this license agreement, other forms of the Software which are executed indirectly, such as an AutoCad ".EXP" form of the Software, are also considered to be DLL Software.

2.   **Sub-License**

You may use the DLL Software under Licensed Software Environments with, and only with, the Distributable Software provided by the CodeBase++ 5 LICENSEE. You may not use the DLL Software for any other purpose. Specifically, you agree not to use the DLL Software for the purposes of developing or creating Executable Software.

3.   **Transfer Restrictions**

The DLL Software is sub-licensed to you, and may not be transferred to anyone without the prior consent of the CodeBase5++ DLL LICENSEE. Any authorised transferee of the sub-license shall be bound by the terms of this agreement.

4.   **Disclaimer**

The DLL Software is provided "as is" without any kind of warranty. It is your responsibility to determine whether the DLL Software is suitable for your purpose.

5.   **Miscellaneous**

This agreement is governed by the laws of the Province of Alberta, Canada. The CodeBase++ SUB-LICENSEE consents to jurisdiction in the province of Alberta, Canada.

Acknowledgements

There are many people who have given life to Life Form and who deserve thanks for their hard work and dedication. We'd like to thank the development team–Steven Overson, Kevin Crenshaw, Ethan Barnes, Nickii Storkus, and Mike Gallacher–for their teamwork and programming prowess. We're grateful to Tom Andrus for his many hours of research and database development, to Jenni Larson for her work with foods and recipes, and Anne Andrus for this manual. We appreciate the work of Mark Hamilton, Dan Baker, and Gary Rasmussen, and the professional advice of Ed Burke and John Allen. We thank Amy Wohl for her comments and suggestions and our many beta sites for their input. Without these people, Life Form could not have become a reality.

CONTENTS

Contacting Fitnesoft

If you have any questions about Life Form, you can look for answers in this manual or using the program's on-screen help. If you cannot find an answer, we encourage you to contact us for help. You can reach Fitnesoft by phone Monday through Friday from 9:00 am to 5:00 pm Mountain time at (801) 221-7708. Be prepared to give the support operator your registration number, as shown on the registration card included in the product box. You're also welcome to contact us by fax, mail, or e-mail at the following addresses and numbers:

Via Mail: Fitnesoft, Inc.
            11 East 200 North, Suite 204
            Orem, UT 84057

Via Phone: (801) 221-7708

Via Fax: (801) 221-7707

Via E-mail:
   For information   info@fitnesoft.com
   For support   support@fitnesoft.com

On the Internet: www.fitnesoft.com

Please feel free to contact us with any comments or suggestions you might have for future versions of Life Form.

Preface

After leaving WordPerfect Corporation in March of 1992, one of my goals was to improve my health. At that time I was an overweight, middle-aged, out of shape, burned out, ex-bigshot, suffering from nightly indigestion and insomnia.

For the next six months I ate a low-fat diet and played tennis five times a week. In spite of these efforts, by the fall I had gained 11 pounds and was less than a quarter inch from having to go to the big and tall shop (and not because I was tall). The experience left me disappointed and frustrated. I had followed the best and most current advice, and had failed miserably.

I came to the conclusion that my health problems were more complicated than I had expected, and decided that what I needed was a software package to help me track my diet, exercise, and other health information. I hoped that the computer could help me figure out how to look and feel better.

After ordering and using the programs available at that time, I ended up disappointed with the results. Either the programs lacked some necessary features, or they were too hard to use. I also did not want a program that told me what to do. I already knew there were no easy answers, and certainly no one-size-fits-all answers. Given that I was fighting time, genetics, and gravity (three very powerful forces), I was more interested in a quick and easy way to keep and view my health information rather than a lot of advice. I was already getting plenty of advice. I needed a way to find out what advice worked for me and what didn't.

Eventually I talked my wife into using part of our savings to hire the programmers and staff necessary to design and write the program I wanted. (Hiring a cook and a personal trainer would have been a lot less expensive, but I was too desperate to think things through very well.)

The project has been an interesting experience. Although I am still overweight and middle-aged, I have discovered how to cure my indigestion. If I watch my simple carbohydrates, primarily sugar and flour, I can avoid the indigestion completely. Getting rid of the indigestion helps my insomnia. I also learned that my blood pressure stays in a mid-normal range, rather than a high normal range, when I exercise regularly and avoid sugar and white flour.

It's too early to tell how much the program will help me with my weight, but I'm hopeful. At the very least, I'll have an accurate medical record so I can show my doctor the results of his advice. I may also find the motivation to make better health decisions.

It is my hope that Life Form will help you learn more about yourself, so that you and your health professionals can discover what you can do to feel and look your best.

W. E. Pete Peterson
Chairman, Fitnesoft, Inc.
May, 1995

Disclaimer

As you use the product, we caution you to remember that while the information we have collected is valid, it may not be completely accurate. Our sources are subject to limitations, as is the data Life Form presents to you. Life Form is intended to be a recordkeeping tool and should not replace the advice of your doctor or other health professional. Before you make any decision that could affect your health, you should consult your doctor.

GETTING STARTED

Welcome to Life Form. Now that you've peeled off the shrink-wrap and cracked open the manual, it's time to get down to the business of taking control of your health. Before you begin using the program, you will need to install it on your computer's hard disk and set up your personal user information. You can read this chapter to learn how to perform the following tasks:

Install Life Form.
Enter and exit the program.
Create a new user.
Switch from one user to another.
Move through the various sections of the program.

It will also introduce you to the Life Form interface and explain the basic Windows skills you need to use the program.

Installing Life Form

Before you install Life Form, you need to make sure your computer has everything necessary to run the program. To use Life Form you need an IBM 386 (or higher) or 100% compatible computer with at least 4MB of RAM and a VGA or better monitor. Your hard disk must have at least 8MB of free disk space, and your computer should be running Windows version 3.1 or later. If your system is missing any of these elements, you will not be able to run Life Form.

When you are ready to install Life Form, follow these steps:

✍ See Windows Skills 1 and 2 for help with starting Windows and using menus.

1.   *(If you are running Windows 3.1)* From the Windows Program Manager File menu, choose Run. *(If you are running Windows 95)* From the Start menu, choose Run.

2.   In the Command Line box, type **a:install** if the disk is in Drive A, or **b:install** if the disk is in Drive B.

✍ See Windows Skills 3 if you don't know how to click.

3.   Click on the OK button.

4.   Follow the instructions on the screen.

(Note: For more information on Life Form's installation options, click on the Help button in the installation dialog.)

WINDOWS SKILL 1 — STARTING WINDOWS

If you are in DOS, you need to start Windows before you can install or use Life Form. To start Windows from DOS, type *win* at the c:\ prompt, then press Enter. If this doesn't work, you need to get help from someone who understands how to start Windows. *(Note: If your computer is running Windows 95, Windows starts automatically.)*

WINDOWS SKILL 2 — USING MENUS

Directly below the title bar (the topmost bar in a window) Windows displays the names of menus in the menu bar. To open a menu, click on its title in the menu bar. To select an option from the menu, click on it. (If you don't know how to click, see *Windows Skill 3 — Clicking.*)

Starting Life Form

Now that you've installed Life Form, you're ready to start the program. If you've just finished installing the program, the Life Form group window will be open and you can double-click on the Life Form icon to start the program. Then skip to Step 2. If the Life Form window is not open, do the following:

✍See Windows Skills 4 if you don't know how to double-click.

1.   (*If you are using Windows 3.1*) From the Windows Program Manager, double-click on the Life Form icon. Then double-click on the new Life Form icon.

(*If you are using Windows 95*) From the Start menu, choose Programs. Then from the Programs submenu, choose Life Form. From the Life Form submenu, choose Life Form again.

2.   If no users have been entered (which is the case if you are opening the program for the first time), the New User dialog box appears. See *Adding a New User* for instructions on entering information in the New User dialog box.

✍See Windows Skills 5 for instructions on changing the time and date.

3.   Check the Status bar to see if the time and date are correct. If they're not, change them in the Windows Control Panel. (You don't need to do this every time you start the program, but it's important that the time and date are correct for your data to be accurate.)

WINDOWS SKILL 4 — DOUBLE-CLICKING

Initially a tricky skill to acquire, double-clicking lets you open and close files and programs. It also provides a shortcut for executing a series of single-click commands. A double-click is two quick taps of a mouse button. If you are new to Windows, you will soon learn that to qualify as a double-click, the clicks of the left mouse button must be made in rapid succession. If you hesitate between clicks, they become two single-clicks rather than a double-click.

WINDOWS SKILL 5 — CHANGING THE TIME AND DATE

Life Form displays the current time and date in the Status bar at the bottom of the Life Form window. The program uses the date and time when you enter information on the various pages. Before you begin using Life Form, you should be sure your computer has the correct time and date. If it doesn't, you can change them by following these steps:

1. If you are using Windows 3.1, from the Program Manager window, double-click on the Main icon. If you are using Windows 95, from the Start menu choose Settings. *(Hint: If you are already in Life Form and using Windows 3.1, you can press Alt+Tab to move to the Program Manager. You may need to press these keys more than once. If you are using Windows 95, press Ctrl+Esc to get to the Start menu. Again, you might need to press these keys more than once.)*
2. From the Main window or the Settings submenu, choose Control Panel. Then, if you are using Windows 95, from the Control Panel submenu, choose Control Panel again. The Control Panel window appears.
3. Double-click on the Date/Time icon. The Date & Time dialog box appears.
4. If the month is incorrect, type the number of the current month or click on the up or down arrow to change the month. In Windows 95 you can choose the month from the list box. If the month is correct, press Tab to move to the next field. Correct the day and the year using these same techniques. Then press Tab to move to the time.
5. If the time is incorrect, type in the correct hour or click on the up or down arrow to change the hour. Then tab to the minutes area. Correct the minutes and the AM/PM setting if they are incorrect. Then press Tab. The focus moves to the OK button.

6. Press Enter or click on the OK button. Windows changes the time and date based on your corrections and returns to the Control Panel window.

7. If you are using Windows 3.1, double-click on the Control-Menu box, located in the upper left corner of the window. If you are using Windows 95, click on the close box in the upper right corner of the window. This closes the Control Panel window. You can see *Windows Skill 12 — Closing Windows* for more information on closing windows. (*Hint: If you began from Life Form as noted in Step 1, you can press Alt+Tab or Ctrl+Esc to return to the program.*)

Adding a New User

The first time you open the program, or any time no user exists, the New User dialog box appears. You can add a user by following these steps:

1. Make sure the New User dialog box appears on the screen. If it doesn't, choose New from the File menu, or type Ctrl+N.

✍See Windows Skills 6 for information on keyboard short-cuts.

2. Enter your name in the Name text box, then press Tab.

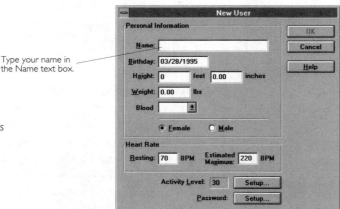

Type your name in the Name text box.

✍See Windows Skills 7 for tips on entering data in Windows.

3. Enter your birthday, then press Tab.

✍ See Windows Skills 8 for more information on text boxes.

4. Enter your height and weight, then press Tab.

5. Choose your blood type from the Blood Type list, then press Tab. If you don't know your blood type, choose *Unknown*. Choosing *Unknown* will not affect your data in any way.

6. Choose your sex by clicking on the Female or Male radio button. Female is already selected, so if you are a female, you can tab through to the Resting Heart Rate box.

7. Edit your resting heart rate if you know it. Then press Tab.

    Life Form assigns all users a resting heart rate of 70. This number represents an average for the general adult population. You can come up with a more accurate estimate by measuring it yourself. To measure your resting heart rate, find your pulse on your neck or wrist with your middle finger. (You should do this while you are resting and your heart rate is not elevated from physical activity. Count the number of beats for 10 seconds, and multiply the number by 6.)

8. Press Tab to move through the Estimated Maximum Heart Rate box, unless you want to edit this information.

    Your maximum heart rate is defined as the highest heart rate your body can attain. Life Form calculates your estimated maximum heart rate using the following formula:

    Maximum Heart Rate = 220 - age

    This formula is recognized by many in the medical community as an accurate estimate for most people. While a doctor can estimate your maximum heart rate more closely under supervised conditions, you should not attempt to measure it yourself. To do so could put undue strain on your body and present a possible danger to you. You can, however, determine that the calculated number is too low if your pulse exceeds it when you exercise. If you believe your maximum heart rate to be different than the result of this formula, you can edit the calculated number by typing over it.

✎Life Form uses your Activity Level to estimate the number of calories you burn daily.

9. You now need to set up your Activity Level. Life Form assigns you an Activity Level based on the information you provide in the Activity Level Setup. The program uses this number in estimating how many calories you burn each day. To set your Activity Level, click on the Activity Level Setup button. The Activity Level Setup dialog box then appears.

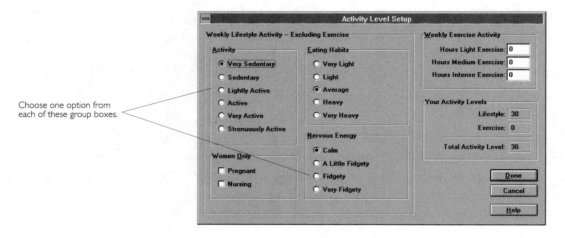

Choose one option from each of these group boxes.

✎See Windows Skills 9 for help with radio buttons.

10. Choose an Activity rating by clicking on one of the Activity radio buttons. Then press Tab.

The option you choose should reflect your general lifestyle excluding exercise, or in other words, your activity at work and at home. Life Form automatically assigns you a *Very Sedentary* rating unless you select another option. Use the following explanations and examples as a guideline for selecting your personal rating:

Very Sedentary. You should choose this rating if you avoid all types of physical activity, including getting up to answer the phone or turn off the TV.

Sedentary. You should choose this rating if you spend most of your day sitting at a desk or on a couch and don't get up much. Examples of sedentary professions are computer programmer and telephone operator.

Lightly Active. You should choose this rating if you spend a good part of your day on your feet. Examples of lightly active professions are floor salesman and nurse.

Active. You should choose this rating if you spend most of your day on your feet or engaged in moderate physical activity such as walking short distances. Examples of active professions are mailman, maid, and waitress.

Very Active. You should choose this rating if you spend most of your day engaged in heavy physical activity, such as walking long distances or lifting and carrying boxes. If you are very active, you break a sweat during your daily activities. Examples of very active professions are carpenter, meatpacker, and carpet layer.

Strenuously Active. You should choose this rating if you spend most of your day engaged in very heavy physical activity, such as running or carrying heavy objects. You are strenuously active if you not only break a sweat but also breathe hard during your activity. Examples of strenuously active professions are lumberjack and bicycle courier.

11. If you are a woman and pregnant or nursing, click on the appropriate check box in the Women Only group box. Then tab to the Eating Habits group box.

12. Select an Eating Habits rating by clicking on one of the Eating Habits radio buttons. Then press Tab.

Life Form assumes you are an *average* eater, or that you consume approximately 2000 calories per day if you are a woman and 2500 calories per day if you are a man. If, however, you eat significantly more or less than the average person of your gender, you should choose one of the other Eating Habits options. If you eat infrequently or only in very small amounts, you should classify yourself as a *very light* eater. If you consume more than a very light eater, but less than an average eater, you qualify as a *light* eater. If you eat more often or in greater amounts than the average person, you are considered a *heavy* eater. If you eat extra-large portions and possibly four to five full meals per day, you should classify yourself as a *very heavy* eater.

13.   Select a Nervous Energy rating by clicking on one of the Nervous Energy radio buttons. Then press Tab.

If you continually exhibit nervous energy by fidgeting, you should choose *Very Fidgety* from the list of options. If you are frequently, but not always, restless or fidgety you should choose *Fidgety*. If you get a little antsy every now and then, but for the most part are relaxed, you should choose *A Little Fidgety*. If you describe yourself as generally relaxed, choose *Calm* from the list.

14.   Enter the number of hours you spend each week doing light, medium, and intense exercise. If you enter these numbers, Life Form will calculate exercise calorie expenditures from this estimate as well as from the actual exercises you enter on the Exercise page. Examples of *light* exercises are golf, bowling, and average walking. *Medium* exercises include fast walking, badminton, and dancing. Examples of *intense* exercises are running, aerobics, and cross-country skiing.

Note: For an explanation of each of the Activity Level Setup options and the methods used in calculating Activity Level, see the **Notes** *section of* **Chapter 4, Exercise**.

15.   When you have completed the setup, choose Done.

16.   If you want to protect your file with a password, set up a password following the steps described in *Password Protecting Your Data* later in this chapter.

17.   Choose OK. Life Form creates a file under the name you entered in the Name text box.

WINDOWS SKILL 6 — USING KEYBOARD SHORTCUTS

Like many other programs, Life Form provides you with keyboard equivalents for choosing commands. These shortcuts involve the Alt and Ctrl keys as described below.

Alt Keys. Each Life Form menu and dialog box option contains an underlined letter. To choose an option, hold down the Alt key while pressing its underlined letter key. For example, to display the File menu, press Alt+F.

Control Keys. Some commands can be executed without opening the menus that contain them. You can choose commands by pressing the Control key in conjunction with another assigned key. For example, to create a new user, press Ctrl+N.

WINDOWS SKILL 7 — ENTERING DATA IN WINDOWS

While not all Windows programs work exactly the same way, most use some common keystrokes to help you enter data.

Click. You can click the left mouse button to move the cursor to an area where you want to enter data. If you position the pointer between characters that have already been entered and then click, the cursor appears between the characters. Any new characters you type are inserted between the existing characters.

Double-Click. Double-clicking is helpful when you want to highlight an entire field so you can delete old information and enter new information. When you double-click on a field, all the characters in the field are highlighted. Once you begin typing, the old characters are deleted.

Left and Right Arrow Keys. You can use the left and right arrow keys to move the cursor within blocks of text. Each time you press the left arrow key, the cursor moves one character to the left. Each time you press the right arrow key, the cursor moves one character to the right.

Del and Backspace. The Del and Backspace keys let you delete characters when entering or editing data. When you press the Del key, you delete the character to the right of the cursor. When you press the Backspace key, you delete the character to the left of the cursor.

Tab and Shift+Tab. Tab and Shift+Tab help you move between fields of data and different areas of dialog boxes. When you press the Tab key, the cursor moves forward one field. When you press the Tab key while holding down the Shift key, the cursor moves back one field or area.

Shift+Arrow Keys. Pressing one of the four arrow keys while holding down the Shift key gives you an easy way to highlight areas of text. You can highlight one character at a time by holding down the Shift key and pressing the right or left arrow key. You can highlight full or partial lines of text by pressing the up or down arrow key while holding down the Shift key.

Ctrl+Arrow Keys. You can use the Ctrl key in conjunction with the four arrow keys to move between fields in a dialog box or different areas of a window. If you hold down the Ctrl key and press the right arrow key, the cursor moves to the next word in a field. Pressing the left arrow key while holding down the Ctrl key moves the cursor to the previous word. When you hold down the Ctrl key and press the up or down arrow, the cursor moves up or down from record to record in a window.

Ctrl+Enter. You might become frustrated if you are typing in a field and want to start a new paragraph. If you press Enter, the cursor moves to a new record instead of starting a new line in the field. To start a new line in a record, press Enter while holding down the Ctrl key.

WINDOWS SKILL 8 — USING TEXT BOXES

Text boxes are boxes into which you type requested information. To activate a text box, click on it. Then type your selection.

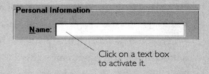

Click on a text box to activate it.

WINDOWS SKILL 9 — USING RADIO BUTTONS

Radio buttons, also known as option buttons, are round and are used when you need to choose a single option from a group of options. The radio button for an option is shaded when the option is selected, and empty when it is not. To select a radio button, click on it. You can also use the arrow keys to move between radio buttons in a group of options. In the dialog box below, the *Calm* button is selected.

Click on a radio button to select it.

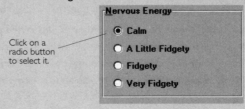

The rectangular buttons that appear in every dialog box are called command buttons. For purposes of the *User's Guide*, a command button will be referred to as a *button*. You click on a button to initiate an action such as canceling or confirming information you have entered. In any group of command buttons, the button with the darker, heavier border is called the default. You can select the default by pressing Enter instead of clicking on it. For example, pressing Enter in the dialog box below selects the OK button and confirms the entered information.

New Exercise

Exercise Name: [   ]

Default Units: [   ] ±

Default Intensity: [1.00]

OK

Cancel

Help

Click on a button to execute a command.

Password Protecting Your Data

If you do not want other people to have access to your data, you can protect your information with a password. Before Life Form will open a password protected file, it requires the user to enter the password associated with the file. By setting up a password, you can insure the privacy and accuracy of your personal information (although a very clever person can sometimes defeat this protection). Setting up a password is optional, and you probably won't want to if you're not worried about other people viewing your data. If you password protect your data and then forget the password, you will not be able to see your information. If you decide you want to use a password, follow these steps:

1.   In the New User dialog box, click on the Password Setup button. The Password Setup dialog box appears.

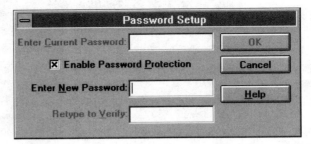

2. Enter a password of up to 15 characters, and press Tab. (You will not see the password as you type it. Instead, you will see an asterisk in place of each character.)

3. Retype the password in the Retype to Verify text box.

4. Choose OK to return to the New User dialog box. If the passwords typed in Steps 2 and 3 do not agree, Life Form displays this error message:

If this message appears, choose OK and repeat Step 3 until the passwords match and Life Form returns to the New User dialog box.

*Note: You can change your password at any time as long as you remember it. See **Editing a User** later in this chapter for more information.*

Moving from Page to Page

Moving between Life Form's eight pages is as easy as a click of the mouse. Each page is represented by a tab located directly below the menu bar. Unless you reduce the size of Life Form's program window, all eight tabs appear at all times. If you have a color monitor, the top of each tab is a different color. The lower section of the tab for the active page is white, while the bottoms of the other seven tabs remain gray.

The Information page is active.

The Exercise page is not active.

✍️*Or select the name of the page from the Page menu.*

To move from one page to another, click on the tab of the page you want to see. (You can also select the name of the page from the Page menu.) Life Form saves information as you enter it, so you are not at risk of losing any data by changing pages. If you click on the gray area to the right of the tabs, Life Form displays the Title page, the blank page that appears if a feature page is not selected.

Note: If the size of the program window is not wide enough to accommodate all eight tabs, an Index tab appears. To move to a page for which a tab does not appear, click on the Index tab and select the page from the list.

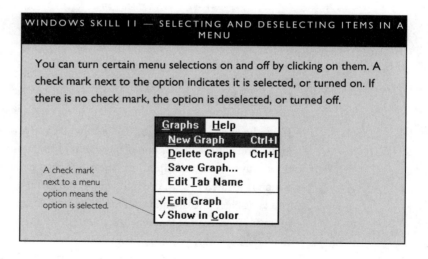

Using the Status Bar

✍️*See Windows Skills 11 for help with selecting or deselecting a menu option.*

The Status bar appears on the Life Form screen unless you turn it off by deselecting it in the View menu. The left end of the bar displays help information or status information about commands and selections. If you do not want to see these messages, deselect the Status Messages option in the View menu. Life Form displays the current date and time in the center of the bar. The right end of the bar is reserved for buttons that provide shortcuts for changing users and printing and deleting selected information.

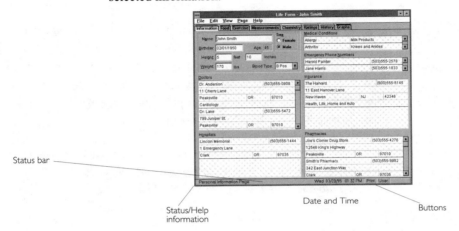

Status bar

Status/Help
information

Date and Time

Buttons

Using Help

If you have questions about Life Form while you are using the program, you can use the online help system to find answers. There are three ways to access help information. The first is the Help menu, which is located toward the right end of the menu bar. From this menu you can select one of eight options. *Windows Tutorial* is a short program from Microsoft that teaches you basic Windows skills. It is particularly helpful if you aren't sure how to use the mouse. *About Life Form* shows you basic facts about the program such as copyright date and trademark information. *Contents* opens the main help system and lets you look for help information from a table of contents. *Search for Help On* lets you search for information by entering keywords or scrolling through a list of topics. For more information on the Contents and Search for Help On options, select *How to Use Help* from the Help menu. *Current Page* opens the help system for the page of the program you are working in. *Contacting Fitnesoft* provides you with phone numbers and electronic addresses you can use to contact the maker of Life Form. *Readme* contains information on recent changes to the program that might not be reflected in the manual.

The second way to access help information is to press F1, the help key, for context-sensitive help. When you press F1, Life Form opens a Contents menu for the current page.

If you want more information on the options provided in a dialog box, Life Form offers you a third way to find help information. Each dialog box in Life Form has a Help button, like the one in the dialog box shown here.

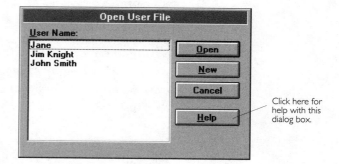

Click here for help with this dialog box.

When you press the button, information regarding the dialog box appears.

If you cannot find the answers to your questions using the online help system, you can refer to this manual or contact Fitnesoft's support operators. For information on contacting Fitnesoft see *Contacting Fitnesoft* on p. ix.

Backing Up Your Data

Because data can be lost or corrupted due to hard disk errors, Life Form gives you an easy way to back up your information onto a floppy disk. When you use the Backup feature, Life Form saves a copy of each user's data to the disk and directory you specify. While you can back up data to your hard disk, we strongly recommend you back up to a floppy disk. This way you can be sure you have an additional copy of your data that will not be affected if your hard disk fails. To back up your Life Form data, follow these steps:

1. Insert your backup disk into the floppy drive. (Because backing up may require more than one disk, you should have a number of blank, formatted disks available.)

✍ Or type Ctrl+B.

2. From the File menu, choose Backup. The Backup dialog box appears.

3. If you want to back up files to a directory or drive other than a:\lifeform.bak, enter the name of the directory or drive. You can use the Browse button to search for an alternate location.

    Note: If you do not change this setting, Life Form assumes you want to save the information to a floppy disk in your computer's a:\ drive. The program creates a **lifeform** directory on the floppy disk if one does not already exist.

4. If you want to proceed with a standard installation, choose Finish. If you want to view more backup options, choose Next.

5. Choose the type of backup you want Life Form to perform. If you leave the Full option selected, Life Form includes all files for all users you select in the backup. (You can select users in the next dialog.)

    If you choose Minimal, Life Form omits all the files it can rebuild from the backup. This includes all the "cdx" files (database index files) and *calc.dbf* and its associated files. Although the Minimal option is much faster while backing up, it is much slower when restoring. We recommend you use the minimal option only for emergency recovery of data.

    You can select the Users' Foods option to back up the databases of foods and recipes added or edited by users. You might want to do this if you are transferring foods between machines. If, for example, you added a group of recipes on your machine that your friend would like on his, you can back up your users' food databases and then restore them to your friend's machine. For more information on restoring the users' food databases, see *Restoring Data from a Backup* later in this chapter.

6.   Choose Finish to begin the backup or Next for more options.

7.   If you chose the Full or Minimal option in Step 5, choose the users you want to back up. To back up all users, select the All Users option. To select a user or users, choose the Selected Users option and click on the name of the user(s) in the list. *(Note: If you select this option, you must select at least one name from the list by clicking on it. If no users are selected from the list, you cannot continue with the backup.)*

8.   Choose Finish.

9.   If you have previously backed up data to the floppy disk's *lifeform* directory, Life Form asks if you want to replace the old backup. If you want to copy the new backup over the old one, choose OK. If not, choose Cancel and return to Step 1.

10.   Life Form displays the Backup Status dialog box. You can cancel the backup by clicking on the Cancel button.

11.   If the data fills more space than is available on the floppy disk, Life Form prompts you to insert another disk. At the prompt, eject the old disk and insert a new one. Then press OK to continue the backup. You may need to repeat this process more than once if you are backing up a lot of users or have been using the program for a long time. If this is the case, be sure to number the disks as you use them, for example, *Backup 1*, *Backup 2*, etc.

Life Form informs you when the backup is complete.

12.   Choose OK to return to the program window.

Restoring Your Data From a Backup

If your hard disk fails or somehow loses data, you will want to restore
your data from your backup disk(s). Before you do, you will need to
reinstall Life Form. To do this, refer to *Installing Life Form* earlier in
this chapter. Once you have reinstalled the program, you can follow
these steps to restore your data:

✐Or type Ctrl+R.

1.   Insert your first backup disk.

2.   From the File menu, choose Restore. The Restore dialog box
       appears.

3.   If you want to restore the data from a drive or directory other
       than the one displayed, enter the name of the drive or directo-
       ry. Then choose OK. You can use the Browse button to search
       for possible backup locations.

4.   Choose Finish to begin the restoration or Next for more
       options.

5.   Choose which data you want to restore. Life Form displays
       the users included in the backup in the list box. You can
       choose All Users to restore data for all users from the backup.
       You can choose specific users by choosing Selected Users and
       clicking on the names in the list. *(Note: You must choose at
       least one user from the list if this option is selected or you will
       not be able to proceed with the backup.)* Any existing user
       with the same name as a user on the backup will be replaced.
       If the backup contains a user that is not found on the hard

drive, the user will be added to the existing group of users.

6. Choose Finish to begin the restoration or Next to view more options.

7. Specify what you want Life Form to do with the data from the users' food databases. If you choose the Merge option, Life Form merges the users' food databases from the backup with the current users' food databases. If the databases contain foods with the same name but different ingredients or nutritional information, Life Form displays the Food Conflict Dialog. (For more information on this dialog, use the online help system.)

   If you choose the Replace option, Life Form replaces the current users' food databases with the databases from the backup. You might want to use this option if you need to restore Life Form to a previous state due to a hardware or software failure.

   If you choose Keep, Life form keeps the current users' food databases and disregards the databases from the backup. You might want to use this option if you have entered data on another computer but do not want to make any changes to the current users' food databases.

8. Choose Finish to begin the restoration.

9. If you have entered any data since installing the program, Life Form displays a warning. If you want to replace the existing data with the backup data, choose OK.

10. The Restore Status dialog box appears. You can cancel the restoration by clicking on the Cancel button. Once the restoration is complete, Life Form returns to the program window.

   Life Form informs you when it has finished restoring your data.

10. Choose OK to return to the program window.

Note: When you restore data from a backup, Life Form over-writes the current data with the backup data. You will lose any data you have entered for any user since the backup was made. In other words, if you have added any users since making the backup, you will lose all their data including their User Setups.

Exiting Life Form

✍See Windows Skill 12 for information on closing a program window.

You can exit Life Form from any page in the program. To exit, select Exit from the File menu. Life Form saves information as you enter it, so you do not need to save files before exiting the program.

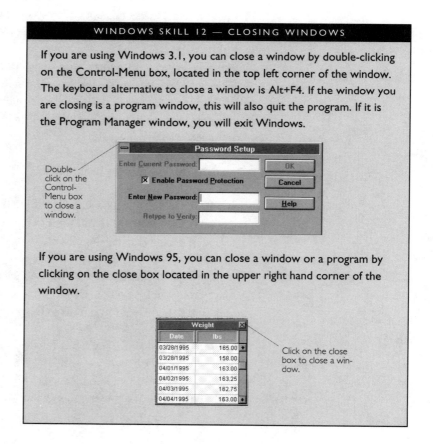

Adding Another User

Life Form lets you add as many users as will fit on your computer's hard disk. To add additional users, follow the steps listed in *Adding a New User*.

Opening a User

When you start Life Form, the program automatically opens the last user to the last page used. If you want to open a different user, follow these steps:

✍*Or type Ctrl+O.*

1. Click on the User button located on the Status bar at the bottom of the screen. (You can also select Open from the File menu.) The Open User File dialog box appears.

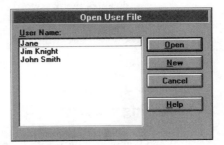

2. Select the name of the user you want to open from the list by clicking on it.

3. Choose Open.

4.   If the file is password protected, the Open Password Protected File dialog box appears. Enter the password at the prompt, then choose OK.

Note: Life Form displays the names of the last four files used at the bottom of the File menu. To open one of these users, click on the user name.

Editing a User

You can edit your User Setup at any time by following these steps:

1.   From the File menu, select Edit User. The Edit User Setup dialog box appears.

2.   Enter any changes or corrections to your name, birthday, height, weight, blood type, sex, resting heart rate, estimated maximum heart rate, or Activity Level in the appropriate fields.

3.   If you want to change your password, click on the Password Setup button. Enter and verify the new password at the prompts.

        If you have set up a password for a file and no longer want to use it, deselect the Enable Password Protection option. This disables the password protection feature.

4.   Choose OK. Life Form records your changes.

Closing a User

✍ *Or type Ctrl+S.*

When you open a user, Life Form automatically closes the previous user. In other words, only one file is open at a time. If you want to close a file without opening another, select Close from the File menu. When you do this, Life Form displays the Title page.

Deleting a User

If you want to delete a user, you should be aware that any data entered in the user's file will be permanently lost. To delete a user, follow these steps:

1.   From the File menu, select Delete. The Delete User dialog box appears.

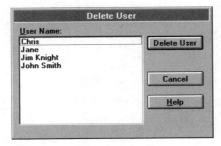

2.   Choose the name of the user you want to delete from the list by clicking on it.

3.   Choose Delete User. Life Form displays a warning.

4.   Choose Yes. Life Form deletes the user and all the data it contains.

Setting Preferences

Life Form lets you customize four different aspects of the program to reflect your personal preferences. To change the setting of one or all four preferences, follow these steps:

1.   From the File menu, choose Preferences. The Preferences dialog box appears.

2.   If you do not want Life Form to open a user on startup, click on the None radio button in the Initial User on Startup group box. If you do not choose this option, Life Form opens to the last user.

3.   If you want Life Form to open to the same page each time you start the program, choose the Title page or one of the eight feature pages from the Initial Page on Startup group box. If you don't select this option, Life Form opens to the last page used.

4.   If you want to record your weight and height in metric units, click on the Metric radio button in the Units for Height, Weight group box. If you do not choose this option, Life Form uses English units— feet, inches, and pounds.

5.   If you want to print your graphs using the orientation selected in the Print Setup, click on the As Specified in Print Setup radio button. If you do not choose this option, Life Form prints graphs in landscape orientation.

6.   When you are finished editing the preferences, choose OK.

If you change your mind about a preference, you can change it back to the previous setting by opening the Preferences dialog box and reselecting the old option.

Changing the Print Setup

If you have problems printing, you should check the Print Setup to make sure a printer is available and selected. To check the Print Setup, click on the Setup button in the Print dialog box. If everything appears to be okay in the Print Setup, you can try printing from another application. If you can print using another program, there could be a problem with Life Form. To contact Fitnesoft about a printing problem, see *Contacting Fitnesoft* on p. ix.

Note: You can refer to your Windows documentation for more information on printing and printers.

Notes

The Life Form Files

Life Form comprises 18 basic files and generates up to 46 additional files for each user. When you install the program, it creates a **c:\lifeform** directory in which it stores all these files, unless you specify otherwise. Most of the files are contained in subdirectories of this master directory. The files listed below are stored in the master directory.

lfdb.dll - database dynamic link library
lifeform.exe - the program's executable file
lifeform.ini - contains initialization information
lifeform.hlp - contains the program's help information

The program contains a variety of database (*.DBF) files, in which it stores information for all of Life Form's predefined items as well as those items added and edited by users. Each database file has a corresponding index (*.CDX) file that helps Life Form search the database for information. Some of the databases also have database transaction (*.TNX) files associated with them. These files monitor the databases files and help to preserve their integrity. The following database files are stored in the **c:\lifeform\users** directory. They contain information shared by all the people using Life Form on your machine.

food.dbf - contains data for Life Form's 13,000+ predefined food items
food_s.dbf - contains data for foods added by users
gvars.dbf - contains setup information for the predefined items from the Exercise, Measurements, Chemistry, and Ratings pages
recipe.dbf - contains names and ingredient lists for 1000+ predefined recipes
recipe_s.dbf - contains names and ingredient lists for recipes added by users
users.dbf - contains information from User Setups

(The **c:\lifeform\users** directory also contains a .CDX file for each of these database files and .TNX files for the **food_s.dbf** and **recipe_s.dbf** files.)

Within the **c:\lifeform\users** directory, Life Form creates individual user subdirectories. The directory for each user can contain any or all of the following database files, depending on the pages the user uses.

calc.dbf - contains calculated data for daily, weekly, and monthly values
food_r.dbf - contains data for recently used foods
food_x.dbf - contains data for deleted foods

graphs.dbf - contains setup information for graphs created by user

grvars.dbf - contains changes to graph settings for items included in graphs

gvars.dbf - contains changes to information for items edited and added by user

history.dbf - contains data entered by user on the History page

meal.dbf - contains date, time, meal type information for meals in user's Meal History

mealitem.dbf - contains names and servings sizes of foods entered in user's meals

persinfo.dbf - contains data entered by user on the Information page

rpt}0000.dbf - temporary file created to generate report from graph data

track.dbf - contains data entered by user on Measurements, Chemistry, and Ratings pages

(Life Form creates a corresponding .CDX and .TNX file for each of these .DBF files.)

Once a user uses one of the program's eight pages, Life Form creates an .RST file under the user's directory. The .RST file enables Life Form to remember the state of the page when the user leaves it and restore it when the user returns to it. The following is a list of the the possible .RST files.

chemistr.rst - remembers and restores the state of the Chemistry page

exercise.rst - remembers and restores the state of the Exercise page

food.rst - remembers and restores the state of the Food page

history.rst - remembers and restores the state of the History page

informat.rst - remembers and restores the state of the Information page

measurem.rst - remembers and restores the state of the Measurements page

ratings.rst - remembers and restores the state of the Ratings page

There are two .FPT files that store the information you enter as notes on the History and Exercise pages.

activity.fpt - stores text entered in Notes field on the Exercise page

history.fpt - stores text entered in Notes field on History page

Finally, Life Form creates an .INI file for each user to store the user's initialization information.

user.ini - stores the user's initialization information

INFORMATION

The Information page lets you store basic details about you and the medical professionals who care for you. Using this page, you can keep track of your current doctors, pharmacies, hospitals, insurance policies, emergency numbers, and special medical conditions. You can easily print your information so you can keep a copy near the phone or leave your children's data with the baby-sitter in case of emergency.

This chapter explains how to enter, edit, delete, and print data using the Information page.

Basic Features

The Information page comprises an area containing your basic information and six different entry form windows. In these windows, you can keep lists of medical information, including doctors, hospitals, medical conditions, emergency phone numbers, insurance carriers, and pharmacies.

Life Form displays basic information about the user from the User Setup.

You enter information about your medical providers in six different windows on the Information page.

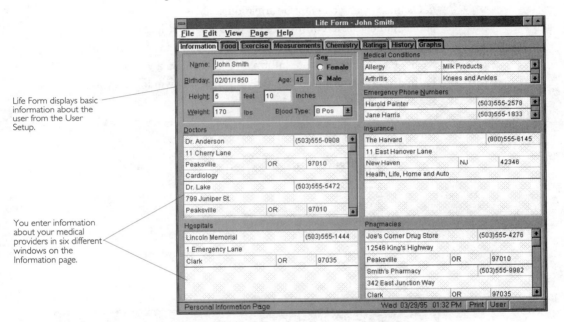

Entering and Editing Basic Information

Life Form stores the data you enter when setting up your user file and copies much of it to the Information page. Your name, sex, birthday, height, weight, and blood type appear in the upper left corner of the page. You can edit any of this information by clicking in the appropriate field and entering your changes. Life Form automatically updates your User Setup when you make changes to this data.

Entering a Record

The Information page lets you save information in six different categories: doctors, hospitals, medical conditions, emergency phone numbers, insurance, and pharmacies. Each of these categories is represented by a *window* on the screen. When you click on any of these windows, Life Form displays an *entry form*. Each form contains a series of *fields* into which you enter information such as name, address, and telephone number. Life Form saves the data you enter in these fields as *records* or *entries*. You may add as many records to a category as you wish. Once you enter more information than fits in a window, Life Form displays a scroll bar in the right side of the window so you can see all your records.

✍See Windows Skill 13 for help with scroll bars.

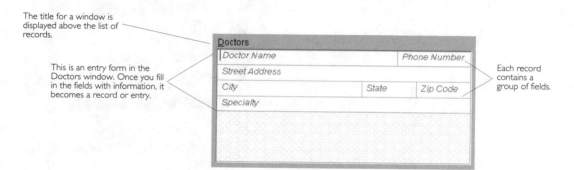

The title for a window is displayed above the list of records.

This is an entry form in the Doctors window. Once you fill in the fields with information, it becomes a record or entry.

Each record contains a group of fields.

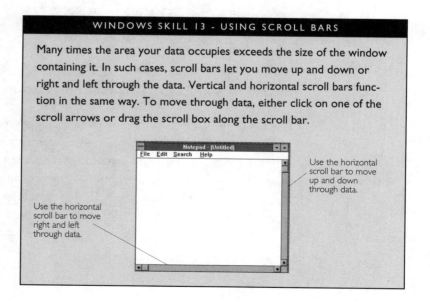

WINDOWS SKILL 13 - USING SCROLL BARS

Many times the area your data occupies exceeds the size of the window containing it. In such cases, scroll bars let you move up and down or right and left through the data. Vertical and horizontal scroll bars function in the same way. To move through data, either click on one of the scroll arrows or drag the scroll box along the scroll bar.

Use the horizontal scroll bar to move up and down through data.

Use the horizontal scroll bar to move right and left through data.

Entering a Doctor

To enter a doctor, follow these steps:

✍Or click anywhere in the Doctors window and type Ctrl+I.

1.	Click on a blank area in the Doctors window so that the entry form appears. If the window is already filled with records, scroll down to the bottom of the list and click in the blank area. (You can also click anywhere in the Doctors window and select Insert Entry from the Edit menu.)

2.	Type the doctor's name and press the Tab key. Type the phone number and press Tab. Continue by filling in the street address, city, state, and zip code in this manner.

3.	Enter the doctor's specialty, for example, podiatry or pediatrics. Then press Tab. Life Form automatically saves the information as a Doctor record.

LIFE FORM TIP

If you make a mistake while entering information, you can use Shift+Tab or click with your mouse to move back to the field you want to change. Once there, you can use your arrow, Backspace, and Delete keys to edit the information. Once the information is the way you want it, press Enter to save your changes.

Entering a Hospital

To enter a hospital, follow these steps:

✐ Or click anywhere in the Hospitals window and type Ctrl+I.

1. Click on a blank area in the Hospitals window so that the entry form appears. If the window is already filled with records, scroll down to the bottom of the list and click in the blank area. (You can also click anywhere in the Hospitals window and select Insert Entry from the Edit menu.)

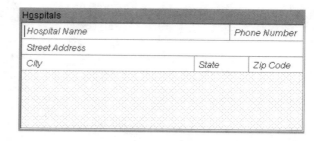

2. Type the hospital name and press the Tab key. Type the phone number and press Tab. Continue by filling in the street address, city, state, and zip code in this manner. Life Form automatically saves the information as a Hospital record.

Entering a Medical Condition

If you have any allergies or conditions that might affect your medical treatment or are important for others to know in emergency situations, you should record them in the Medical Conditions entry form. For example, you might enter your child's allergy to penicillin or note that you are diabetic. To enter a medical condition, follow these steps:

✐ Or click anywhere in the Medical Conditions window and type Ctrl+I.

1. Click on a blank area in the Medical Conditions window so that the entry form appears. If the window is already filled with records, scroll down to the bottom of the list and click in the blank area. (You can also click anywhere in the Medical Conditions window and select Insert Entry from the Edit menu.)

2.   Enter the condition and press Tab to move to the Notes field.

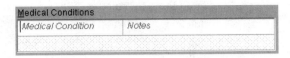

3.   Enter any important related information, such as symptoms or medications used in treating the condition, and press Tab. Life Form stores the information as a Medical Condition record.

Entering an Emergency Phone Number

You can use the Emergency Phone Numbers list to store names and numbers of people or agencies to be contacted in case of emergency. Begin by entering information for your local police and fire departments and poison control hotline. Then add friends and relatives and anyone else you wish to be contacted in emergency situations. To enter an emergency number, follow these steps:

✍Or click anywhere in the Emergency Phone Numbers window and type Ctrl+I.

1.   Click on a blank area in the Emergency Phone Numbers window so that the entry form appears. If the window is already filled with records, scroll down to the bottom of the list and click in the blank area. (You can also click anywhere in the Emergency Phone Numbers window and select Insert Entry from the Edit menu.)

2.   Enter the name of the emergency contact and type Tab. Enter the phone number and type Tab. Life Form stores the information as an Emergency Phone Number record.

Entering an Insurance Plan or Policy

In addition to the Name, Phone Number, Street Address, City, State, and Zip Code fields, Life Form provides a Notes field in the Insurance entry form for storing additional information. To enter insurance data, follow the steps for entering hospitals and pharmacies, then enter any relevant information such as plan titles, group numbers, or policy numbers in the Notes field.

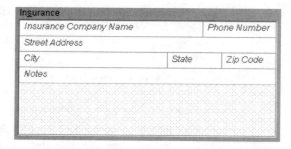

Entering a Pharmacy

Records for pharmacies contain the same basic information as hospital records. You can enter pharmacy information using the steps outlined for entering hospitals.

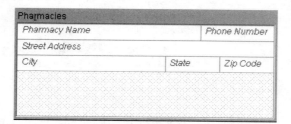

Editing a Record

To edit any of the information entered on the Information page, click on the field you want to edit, type your changes, and press Enter. Life Form automatically stores the most recent changes without you having to press any additional keys.

Deleting a Record

You can delete any record in the Information page by following these steps:

✍Or click on the record and type Ctrl+D.

1. Click on the record and press the Del Entry button in the Status bar. (You can also click anywhere in the record and select Delete Entry from the Edit menu.) The following message appears:

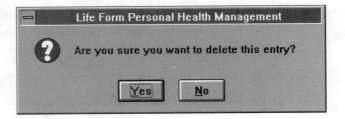

2. Choose Yes. Life Form deletes the record.

Printing the Information Page

When you print the Information page, Life Form prints all the data entered in the six information categories. To print the Information page, follow these steps:

✍Or type Ctrl+P.

1. Click on the Print button on the Status bar. (You can also select Print from the File menu.) The Print dialog box appears.

2. Choose OK. Life Form prints the Information page.

LIFE FORM TIP

If you follow these steps and the Information page does not print, check the Print Setup by clicking on the Setup button in the Print dialog box. For more information on the Print Setup, see *Chapter 1, Getting Started*.

Advanced Features

Copying a User's Information

If you have set up more than one Life Form user on your computer, there's a good chance you and the other user(s) share some common medical information. If you are all family members, you probably use the same insurance carriers, hospitals, and pharmacies, and call the same emergency phone numbers. Once you have entered this information for one user, you can copy it to another user's Information page rather than reentering it. To copy the current user's information to another user's Information page, follow these steps:

1.   From the File menu, choose Copy Info Page. The Copy Information Page dialog box appears.

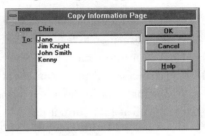

2.   From the list, select the name of the user you want to copy the information to.

3.   Choose OK. Life Form displays the following warning:

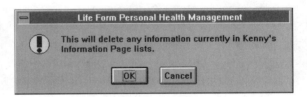

4.   Choose OK. Life Form deletes any information in the selected user's lists and replaces it with the current user's information.

LIFE FORM TIP

If you need to add information to the selected user's lists that is not included in the current user's lists, such as a specific medical condition, wait until you have copied the lists to do so. Any information you enter in the selected user's lists prior to copying will be lost.

Suggestions for Use

Printing Information for the Baby-Sitter

If you've ever used a baby-sitter, you've probably spent time compiling information to leave in case of an emergency. Once you've filled out your Information page, you can print a copy at any time to use in just such an instance. You might want to print your personal data if it contains all the necessary information, or your children's, if you've set them up as Life Form users.

FOOD

If you're like most Americans, you've tried to keep track of the foods you eat at least once in your life. Whether your motivation has been to count calories, track sugar consumption, or evaluate your general nutrition, you've probably found that keeping accurate records is not only time-consuming, but next to impossible. Not with Life Form. By using the Food page, you can track each and every food, calorie, and fat gram you consume without the hassle of searching through tables or charts for data. Life Form contains a database of nutrient values for over 13,000 foods, including many items found on your supermarket's shelves and in your favorite fast food restaurants. You record your meals by selecting foods from this database or adding foods and recipes of your own. You can even edit existing foods to reflect your personal preferences. After you enter your daily meals, Life Form provides you with a breakdown of their calorie and nutrient composition and records them in your personal Meal History. You can review this history from day to day, week to week, or year to year to analyze changes and consistencies in your eating habits.

This chapter explains how to enter meals, create new foods and recipes, use the food detail and nutrition information features, and work within the Meal History. It also contains supplemental information on the new food label, daily reference values, the Life Form food database, and methods for estimating food portions.

Basic Features

The Food page is divided into three sections that make recording your meals and viewing nutrition information easy. The Meal Entry Form, located in the upper left corner of the page, lets you enter the foods you eat by name and serving size. The Nutrition Information window appears in the lower left corner of the page and lets you view basic facts about the nutrition content of your foods. Once you enter meals using the Meal Entry Form, they are saved into the Meal History, located at the right side of the page.

You can enter your meals in the Meal Entry Form.

Life Form stores the meals you enter in the Meal Entry Form in the Meal History.

Life Form displays nutrition information for the foods you enter here.

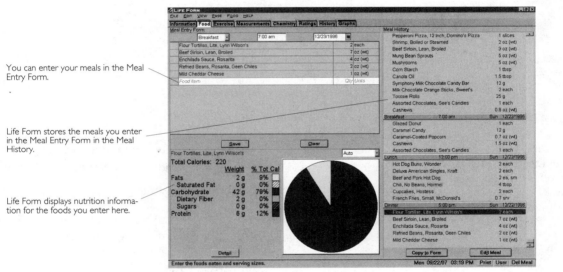

You record your meals by entering the foods you eat in the Meal Entry Form. You can select foods from Life Form's food database, which includes over 13,000 foods found in grocery stores, fast food chains, and restaurants, or you can add your own. The foods in the database fall into two categories: basic foods and recipes. A *basic food* is an individual item for which nutrition information is available in the Nutrition Facts label format. A basic food can be a raw food such as an apple or broccoli, or a manufactured food such as a frozen dinner. Basic foods cannot be broken down into smaller items, even if they contain more than one ingredient. For example, a Big Mac is a basic food even though it is made up of a bun, two hamburger patties, and various condiments.

A *recipe* is a collection of basic foods and possibly other recipes. Life Form calculates Nutrition Facts for recipes by adding the nutrition values of their ingredients. A peanut butter and jelly sandwich is a recipe, because its nutrition values are calculated using the values for three basic foods: peanut butter, jelly, and bread. You can tell a food is a recipe after you enter it in the Meal Entry Form, because the recipe card icon appears to the left of the food name.

A recipe card icon to the left of a food item indicates the food is a recipe.

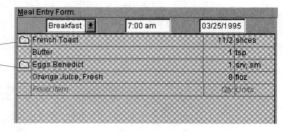

Meal Entry Form		
Breakfast ▼	7:00 am	03/25/1995
French Toast		1 1/2 slices
Butter		1 tsp
Eggs Benedict		1 srv, sm
Orange Juice, Fresh		8 floz
Food Item		*Qty Units*

Entering a Meal

To enter your meals in the Meal Entry Form, follow these steps:

✍ *Life Form automatically displays the type of meal that follows the last meal saved.*

1. From the Meal drop-down list box, select the type of meal you want to enter, and press Tab. You can choose from *Breakfast, Lunch, Dinner*, and *Snack*.

2. Enter the time of the meal if you want, and press Tab. If you do not enter a time for the meal, Life Form assigns one.

3. Enter the date of the meal, and press Tab.

4. Enter the foods in the meal, including quantity and serving size, then press Tab. See *Entering a Food in a Meal* for further instructions on selecting foods, quantities, and serving sizes.

✍ *If you don't want to save the meal, you can press the Clear button to clear the Meal Entry Form.*

5. Once you have entered all the foods for your meal, choose Save. Life Form stores the meal to the Meal History and clears the Meal Entry Form.

Entering a Food in a Meal

To enter a food as part of a meal in the Meal Entry Form, follow these steps:

1. Select a food you have eaten from the Life Form food database.

✎Type specific terms such as brand names to find matches more quickly.

When you begin to type a food in the Food Item field, Life Form searches for it in the food database. As you type more characters, the program reduces the number of records in the search until eventually you have a partial or full match, depending on whether you enter the full food name. Once you find the food, or a suitable match, you can select it. If the match appears highlighted at the top of the list, press Tab to choose it. If it appears farther down in the list, use the down arrow key, click on the food, or continue typing the name exactly as it appears in the list to highlight it. Then press Tab.

Chili Con Carne is selected from the list.

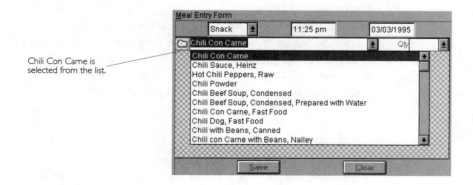

FOOD

Note: If the database does not contain the food you want to enter, you can add it by following the steps outlined in the Adding a New Basic Food or Adding a New Recipe section of this chapter.

2.   Enter the amount you ate in terms of quantity and units. To do this, type a number in the Quantity field, and press Tab. Then select a unit from the drop-down list box, and press Tab again.

For each food, you are given a selection of 24 units of measure. Only some of these units may be relevant for the food you are entering. For suggestions on using these units, see the Life Form Tip immediately following this section.

LIFE FORM TIP

Entering Food Names

When entering a food name in the Food Item field, the easiest way to start is by typing the first thing that comes to mind. You can begin with a flavor, a brand name, a cooking method, a manner of packaging, or a base food name. You don't need to worry about categories, subcategories, or food types, because Life Form's "smart search" calls up food names by matching any word or group of words that you enter. The more you type, the greater the chance the food you're looking for will move to the top of the list.

While the smart search takes the guesswork out of entering food names, there are a few things you can do to speed up the search process. As a rule, you should start with the most specific information you have about the food. Special names attached to foods can be the most specific, such as Big Mac or Special K. Brand names and restaurant names can also be specific, such as Jell-O or McDonald's. Base food names are sometimes less specific, as in the case of gelatin or hamburger. Flavors and manners of preparation and packaging, such as vanilla, baked, and canned, are even less specific.

If you have entered a food item before, Life Form remembers it and assigns it a higher priority in the database than other similar foods. This means the next time you begin to enter the same food, the exact match will appear at the top of the list more quickly.

Entering Quantities

If necessary, you can express the quantity of a food as a fraction, such as 1/2, or a decimal, such as .50. The following example shows a breakfast of 1 1/2 slices of French toast, 1 teaspoon of butter, 3 teaspoons of syrup, 1 small serving of Eggs Benedict, and an 8-fluid ounce glass of orange juice.

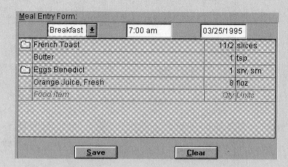

If you ate a prepared food, but left out an ingredient, you can compensate for the change by entering a negative quantity. For example, if you ate a Wendy's Single Hamburger without the pickles, you could enter it as shown below.

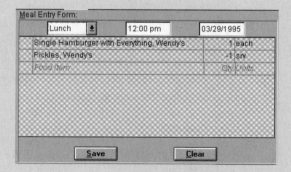

Estimating Serving Sizes

A few of the units in the Units list might be confusing to you. *Each* represents one of the food you have selected. For example, if you enter an apple, an each is one apple. If you enter potato chips, an each is one chip. For some foods, such as lasagna, *each* does not make sense. If you choose each for such foods, the program uses the value for one *serving (srv)*. You can also choose *small each (ea, sm)* or *large each (ea, lrg)* for foods that vary in size, such as oranges, bananas, and carrots.

If you aren't sure how much you ate, you can use the standard serving size as a guideline. Each food record contains data for an average portion as defined by the USDA or food manufacturer. To choose the standard serving, select *srv* from the drop-down list. If you typically eat more or less than the average person, you can choose a *small serving (srv, sm)* or a *large serving (srv, lrg)*.

You can approximate the weight of your foods by comparing them to other foods. We've listed the weights of some common foods below.

Weight	Food
1 g	M & M
3 g	Saltine Cracker
5 g	Grape
1 oz	Strawberry
1.5 oz	Hard Roll
2 oz	Head of Garlic
2.5 oz	Glazed Donut or Lime
5 oz	Lemon
7 oz	Banana or Medium Onion
8 oz	Apple
9 oz	Orange

Often it is easier to estimate a volume measurement for a food rather than a weight. This is because you can estimate visually, based on the amount of space the food fills. You can use the examples listed below as guidelines for estimating volume.

Volume	Item
1 tsp	Large Grape
1 tbsp	Cherry Tomato
1/3 cup	Lime
2/3 cup	Lemon
1 cup	Large Apple
1 1/2 cup	Large Orange
1 fl oz	Shot Glass
6 fl oz	Juice Glass
12 fl oz	Can of Soda
1 qt	32 fl oz Drink

FOOD

Editing a Meal

You can edit a meal any time after saving it by using the Edit Meal button. Whether you left out a food, estimated your portions incorrectly, or simply want to correct some data, you can make changes to any meal in your history at any time. To edit a meal, follow these steps:

1.   In the Meal History, click anywhere in the meal you want to edit.

2.   Click on the Edit Meal button. Life Form displays the meal in the Meal Entry Form.

3.   Make any changes you want to the meal.

4.   Choose Save. Life Form saves the edited meal into the Meal History and clears the Meal Entry Form.

Copying a Meal From the Meal History

Most people fall into patterns with their meals, eating the same things over and over again. We all have our favorite restaurants and recipes, and chances are many of the meals we eat are almost identical from week to week. For some of us, Wednesday is meatloaf day. For others, it's pizza night. In those cases where the meal you are entering is identical or similar to a meal you have previously saved, you can copy a meal from the Meal History to save time. To use a meal already saved in the Meal History, follow these steps:

1. From the Meal drop-down list box, select the type of meal you want to enter, and press Tab.

2. Enter the time of the meal if you want, and press Tab. If you do not enter a time for the meal, Life Form assigns one.

3. Enter the date of the meal, and press Tab.

✍ You can also select an individual food item in a meal by clicking on it.

4. Select the meal you want to copy by clicking on its title in the Meal History.

5. Click on the Copy to Form button located at the bottom of the Meal History. Life Form copies the meal to the Meal Entry Form.

This meal was copied to the Meal Entry Form.

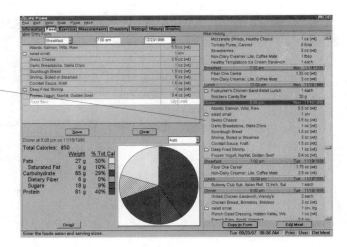

6. If you need to make any changes to the meal, do so following the steps listed in *Entering a Meal*.

7. Choose Save. Life Form saves the meal into the Meal History and clears the Meal Entry Form.

Deleting a Meal

You can delete a meal once you've saved it into the Meal History by following these steps:

1.   Click on the title of the meal you want to delete from the Meal History.

✐*Or type Ctrl+D.*

2.   Click on the Del Meal button in the Status bar. (You can also select Del Meal from the Edit menu.) Life Form displays a warning.

3.   Choose Yes. Life Form deletes the meal from the Meal History.

Viewing Nutrition Information

Life Form offers you two basic ways to view nutrition information for foods contained in the database. The Nutrition Information window, located in the lower left corner of the Food page, displays the nutrient composition of foods, including fats, saturated fat, carbohydrates, dietary fiber, sugars, and protein, both by weight and by percentage of total calories. This information, as well as the number of total calories, appears in columns of text and graphically in a pie chart.

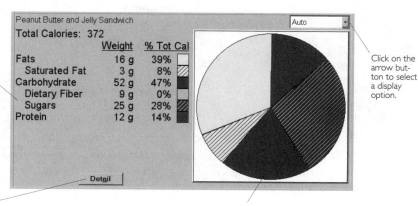

Life Form displays the nutrient composition of foods by weight and percentage of total calories.

Click on the arrow button to select a display option.

You can press the Detail button to view the Nutrition Facts label.

The pie chart displays food composition information graphically.

The Detail button lets you view nutrition information for individual foods and groups of foods in the Nutrition Facts label format. This data for basic nutrients is presented by weight in grams and as a percent daily value for a 2000-calorie diet if you are a woman or for a 2500-calorie diet if you are a man. (*Note: You can customize Life Form to display percent daily values based on your individual diet by using the Daily Nutrition Goals feature. For more information, see **Setting Daily Nutrition Goals** later in this chapter.*)

The Nutrition Facts label includes the weight information presented in the Nutrition Information window as well as serving size by weight or volume, calories from fat, cholesterol, sodium, vitamin A, vitamin C, calcium, and iron. For more information on the Nutrition Facts label, see the *Notes* section of this chapter.

Life Form calculates nutrient values based on the serving size you enter in the Meal Entry Form.

The Food Detail window includes values for the nutrients found on the Nutrition Facts label.

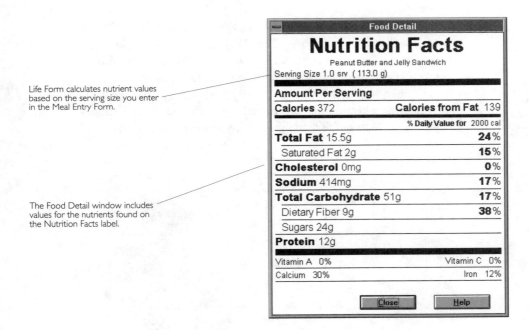

Viewing General Nutrition Information

Life Form displays nutrition information for the foods you eat in the lower left corner of the Food page. Using this window, you can view information for meals, groups of meals, or individual foods after they have been recorded. You have seven options for displaying information — *Auto, Meal, Day, Week, Today, This Week,* and *Last 7 Days*. These options appear in the drop-down list box located directly above the pie chart.

You have seven options for displaying nutrition information.

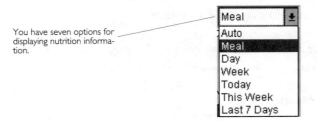

If you leave the setting on *Auto*, Life Form displays information for the last food entered in the Meal Entry Form, or whatever food or meal you have highlighted in the Meal Entry Form or Meal History.

The information for Peanut Butter and Jelly Sandwich appears in the Nutrition Information window.

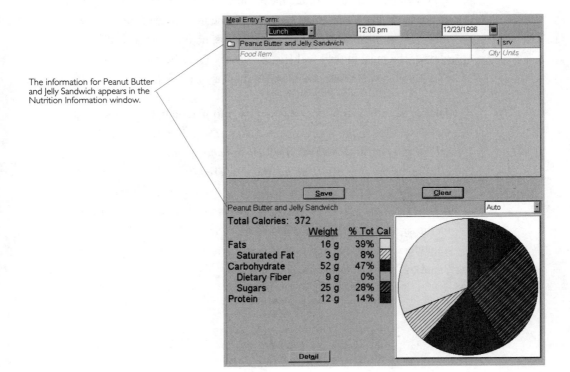

For Individual Foods

Life Form automatically displays nutrition information for the last food entered in the Meal Entry Form. The data that appears is based on the serving size you enter. If the Meal Entry Form is blank, no values appear. You can also view information for an individual food in the Meal History or Meal Entry Form by leaving the display option on *Auto* and clicking on the food entry.

Note: Before you can view the nutrition information for a food, you must select a food name and serving size and then press Tab.

For Meals

Life Form will show you nutrition information for a meal, a day's meals, a week's meals, or meals entered thus far in a calendar week. When you select *Meal* from the list of display options, Life Form shows you information for the meal that currently has the focus. If the cursor is located in the Meal Entry Form, the meal in the form has the focus. If the form is empty but has the focus, no information is displayed. If a meal in the Meal History has the focus because you've clicked on it, the information for that meal is displayed.

The *Day* and *Week* options let you view information based on the meal that is selected in the Meal History. (*Note: There is always a meal selected in the Meal History. If you do not change the selection by clicking on another meal, the last meal entered is the selected meal. The title bar for the selected meal appears in a different color than the title bars for the other meals.*) *Day* displays totals for all meals entered on the same day as the meal selected in the Meal History. *Week* shows totals for all meals entered in the same calendar week (Sunday to Saturday) as the selected meal.

The *Today*, *This Week*, and *Last 7 Days* options let you view information based on the current date rather than the selected meal. *Today* displays totals for all meals you have entered for the current date. *This Week* displays totals for all meals you have entered since the beginning of the calendar week. *Last 7 Days* displays an average of daily totals for the meals you have entered over the last 7 days. If you haven't entered meals on each day, Life Form will calculate the average based on the number of days meals have been entered. If, for example, you entered meals for 5 out of the last 7 days, the values displayed will be the totals divided by 5 rather than 7, or the average values for 5 of the last 7 days. If you choose the Week or This Week option, totals are divided by 7 to get an average, even if you have fewer than 7 days of meals in that week.

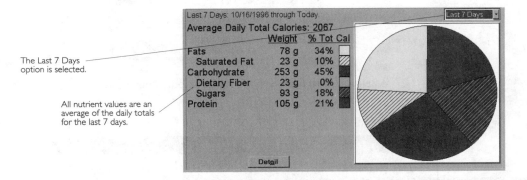

The Last 7 Days option is selected.

All nutrient values are an average of the daily totals for the last 7 days.

Viewing Nutrition Facts

The Detail feature lets you view a greater variety of nutrition information in the more familiar format of the Nutrition Facts label. To view Nutrition Facts using the Detail button, follow these steps:

1. Select a basic food, recipe, meal, or group of meals using the methods described in *Viewing General Nutrition Information*. If you do not change the selection, Life Form displays Nutrition Facts for the current display option.

2.	Click on the Detail button. The Food Detail window appears.

3.	After you have reviewed the information, choose Close.

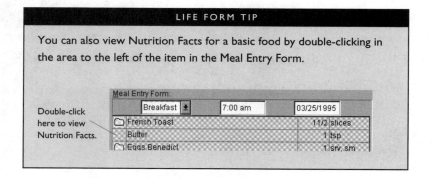

Viewing a Recipe

In addition to viewing Nutrition Facts for a recipe, you can also view its serving size and ingredient information. To view a recipe, follow these steps:

✍ Or type Ctrl+Shift+E.

1. If the recipe you want to view appears as an item in the Meal Entry Form or Meal History, double-click on the recipe card icon to the left of the recipe name and skip to Step 4. Otherwise, select Edit/View Food from the Food menu. The Edit/View Food dialog box appears.

2. Enter the name of the recipe you want to view using the same techniques you use when entering foods in the Meal Entry Form.

3. Click on the View button. The Recipe Card appears.

If you want to edit this recipe, press the Edit button.

4. Choose Close when you are finished viewing the information.

LIFE FORM TIP

If while viewing a recipe you decide you want to edit it, you can click on the Edit button below the ingredient list. This opens the Edit Recipe dialog box. You can then make changes to the recipe by following the instructions provided in *Editing a Food*.

Adding a New Food

If you do not find a food when trying to enter it, you can add it to the food database. Before you add the food, you need to decide whether it is a basic food or a recipe. If the food has a Nutrition Facts label, or the manufacturer has published Nutrition Facts, you can add it as a *basic food*. If you do not have data for a food, but prepared it at home or know its ingredients, you can add it to the database as a *recipe*. To add a new basic food or recipe, follow the steps listed in the next two sections.

Adding a New Basic Food

1. If you are entering foods in the Meal Entry Form and Life Form does not find a match for one of your entries, it displays the following message:

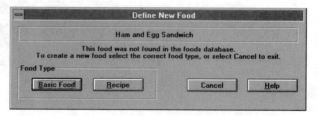

Click on the Basic Food button in the Food Type group box. The New Basic Food dialog box appears.

Copy information from a food's Nutrition Facts label into the New Basic Food dialog box.

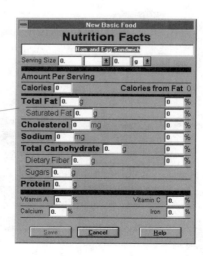

✍Or type Ctrl+Shift+B.

If you are not currently in the Meal Entry Form or did not arrive at the Define New Food dialog, select New Basic Food from the Food menu.

2.   Enter a food name not to exceed 80 characters.

3.   Enter the standard serving size in volume or quantity, and weight.

✍The more information you enter, the more accurate Life Form's calculations will be when you enter the food in the Meal Entry Form.

Most foods bearing the Nutrition Facts label provide values in terms of volume or quantity *and* weight. For example, the Nutrition Facts label on a can of peanuts might display values for a serving size of 28 g, or "about 35 nuts." A label on a box of rice mix might contain information for a serving size of 2 oz, or 1/3 cup. Always enter two values if possible.

4.   Enter the nutrition information as it appears on the food label.

5.   Choose Save.

Note: Basic foods added to the database by one user are available to all users working on the same computer.

Adding a New Recipe

1.   If you are entering foods in the Meal Entry Form and Life Form does not find a match for one of your entries, it displays the following message:

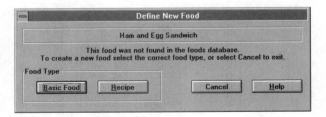

Click on the Recipe button. The Recipe Card dialog box appears.

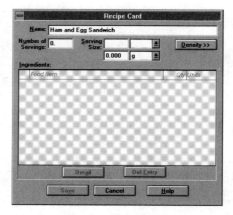

✍Or type Ctrl+Shift+R.

If you are not currently in the Meal Entry Form or did not arrive at the above dialog, select New Recipe from the Food menu.

2. Enter a name for the recipe, then press Tab.

3. Enter the number of servings the recipe makes, then press Tab.

✍You can click on an ingredient and choose Detail to view its Nutrition Facts.

4. Enter the ingredients in your recipe using the same procedure you use to enter foods in the Meal Entry Form. Both basic foods and recipes can be included as ingredients in a recipe.

    Note: If an ingredient does not appear in the database, you need to enter it as a new food before you can enter it in the recipe.

5. Once you have entered your last ingredient, click on the Quantity field of the first serving size line. Enter your most accurate estimate of serving size in terms of each, volume, or weight.

    Your estimate should be made in the unit you will most often use when entering the food in the Meal Entry Form. If, for example, you entered a recipe for peanut butter cookies, you would probably use *each* as the serving size unit. You could then enter the number of cookies you eat in the Meal Entry Form rather than their weight or volume.

Note: If you want to estimate the serving size, but your recipe does not provide this information, consult the Life Form Tip on Entering Foods in this chapter.

6. Enter an alternate serving size in the second Serving Size line if you have an accurate weight estimate.

   Life Form automatically calculates serving size in ounces based on the number of servings you specify and the total weight of the recipe ingredients. These numbers, though accurate for the ingredients before preparation, might not be accurate for the finished product. Therefore, if you know the actual weight of a serving or want to guess, you can edit the calculated weight. You can also enter a volume measurement if you entered an each measurement in the first serving size line.

7. If you want to enter a density estimate, click on the Density button. The Density list appears.

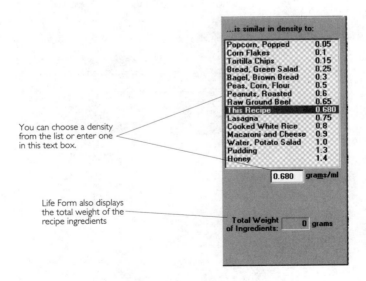

You can choose a density from the list or enter one in this text box.

Life Form also displays the total weight of the recipe ingredients

If you did not enter both a weight and volume measurement in steps 5 and 6, you might want to select a density from the list. If you do, Life Form will make conversions between weight and volume measurements using your estimate rather than the default value.

If you have entered both a weight and volume serving size, Life Form calculates the density of the recipe for you. The calculated number appears in the list as the value for *This Recipe*. You can edit this density if you feel it is not accurate by clicking on another item in the list or entering a new number in the Density text box. Once you edit the density, Life Form may adjust the second serving size to reflect the change.

✎See *Understanding Density* in the *Suggestions for Use* section of this chapter for tips on estimating a density.

8. Choose Save.

Note: Recipes added to the database in one user's file are available to all users working on the same computer.

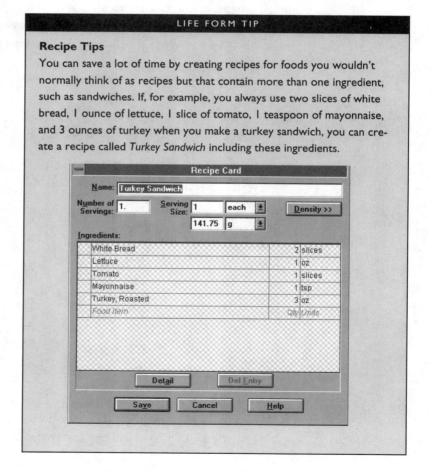

This technique also works well for toast, waffles, pancakes, hamburgers, hot dogs, and other items that include condiments or toppings. This recipe for *My Pancakes* shows that you normally eat 3 pancakes with 2 tbsp of butter and 1/4 cup of maple syrup.

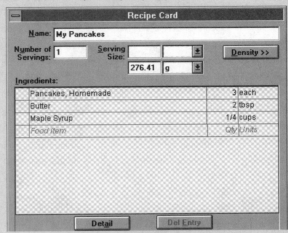

You can take this recipe building technique one step further by creating recipes for meals you eat on a regular basis. If, for example, you eat the same spaghetti dinner every Wednesday night, you can create a recipe like this one:

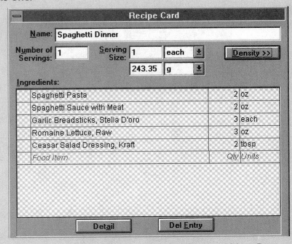

Life Form makes it easy to do this with the Create a New Recipe from Meal feature. For more information see *Creating a New Recipe from a Meal* later in this chapter.

In all the cases we've mentioned thus far, you'll probably want to enter your serving size as *1 each*. By doing this, you are specifying that you usually eat the recipe as a whole, as with a sandwich. In the example of *Turkey Sandwich*, you might enter *1 each* or *.5 each* as the serving size in the Meal Entry Form, depending on whether you ate a whole or half sandwich. If you will consistently use eaches and servings rather than cups, ounces, tablespoons, or any other measurement, you don't need to worry about estimating volume, weight, or density when creating the recipe.

If you are adding a recipe for items such as cookies or muffins, you will also want to use *each* as the basic serving size unit. Be sure to remember though, that unless you want one serving to equal one cookie, you'll need to decide how many cookies make a serving and then figure out the number of servings accordingly. For example, if you want a serving of *Aunt Martha's Peanut Butter Cookies* to equal three cookies and the recipe makes 48 cookies, then the number of servings will be 16 and the serving size will be 3 each.

Recipes can also be used to reflect personal changes to foods already included in the database. If, for example, you prepare a cake using a mix, but use one egg instead of two and leave out 1/4 cup of butter, you can create a recipe like this one:

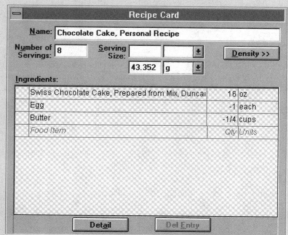

By using the unprepared cake mix as an ingredient and adding each of the additional ingredients you use, you create an alternative to the pre-pared basic food item.

If, on the other hand, you prepare the mix according to the recipe on the box, but add additional ingredients, you can use the prepared item in your recipe as shown here:

Recipe Card		
Name: Chocolate Cake Personal Recipe		
Number of Servings: 8.	**Serving Size:** [ ] 70.038 [g]	**Density >>**
Ingredients:		
Swiss Chocolate Cake, Prepared from Mix, Duncan	16	oz
Chocolate Pudding, Ready-To-Eat	2	oz
Egg	1	each
Food Item	*Qty*	*Units*

| **Detail** | **Del Entry** |

Printing the Food Page

You can print a variety of information from the Food page, including nutrition information for foods and meals, and portions of the Meal History. To print information from the Food page, follow these steps:

✍ *Or type Ctrl+P.*

1.   Click on the Print button in the Status bar. (You can also choose Print from the File menu.) The Print dialog box appears.

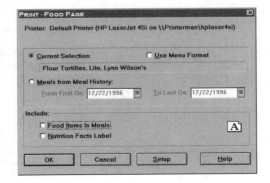

PRINT - FOOD PAGE

Printer: Default Printer (HP LaserJet 4Si on \\Printerman\hplaser4si)

⦿ Current Selection: ☐ Use Menu Format
    Flour Tortillas, Lite, Lynn Wilson's
○ Meals from Meal History:
    From First On [12/22/1996]   To Last On [12/22/1996]

Include:
☐ Food Items In Meals
☐ Nutrition Facts Label

| OK | Cancel | Setup | Help |

FOOD

2. Select the information you want to print by clicking on one of the radio buttons. If you choose *Current Selection*, Life Form will print information for the food, meal, or group of meals currently selected. If you choose *Meals from Meal History*, Life Form will print information for meals contained in a specified date range. If you choose Meals from Meal History proceed to Step 4.

✍The selected item(s) are determined by the display option you have chosen in the Nutrition Information window.

3. If you chose *Current Selection* in Step 2 and the current selection is Auto, Meal, or Day, you have the option of printing your data in menu format. This is a special format that lists the items in each selected meal along with the fat and calories for each item. The data will be printed in portrait orientation and includes a Nutrition Facts label containing nutritional values for the entire selection. To print your data in menu format, check the Use Menu Format checkbox. Then skip to Step 5.

4. If you selected *Meals from Meal History* in Step 2, enter the range of dates you want to print. Enter the beginning date in the From text box and the ending date in the To text box. If you do not edit the dates, Life Form will print information for the last 7 days.

5. If you want to include information for the individual foods in the meals you print, click on the Include Food Items in Meals check box. If you do not select this option, Life Form will print only the total values for each meal.

   Note: *If you selected* **Current Selection** *and the selection is a food item, the Include Food Items option is disabled.*

6. If you want to print a Nutrition Facts label for the selection, check the Include Nutrition Facts Label option.

7. Choose OK. Life Form prints the requested information.

Advanced Features

Editing a Food

Life Form lets you edit any of the basic foods and recipes contained in the food database. Although the data for the original entries is accurate, it is subject to change as food manufacturers revise food labels and publish new nutrition information. If you find that the data on a Nutrition Facts label or manufacturer publication differs from that in the database, you can use the Edit Food feature to change it. You can also edit Life Form's predefined recipes to reflect your personal preferences or change your personal recipes as you change your cooking styles. To edit a basic food or recipe, follow these steps:

✎Or type Ctrl+Shift+E.

1. From the Food menu, select Edit/ViewFood. The Edit/View a Basic Food or Recipe dialog box appears.

2. Enter the name of the basic food or recipe you want to edit using the same techniques you use when entering foods in the Meal Entry Form.

3. Click on the Edit button.

4. Make the necessary changes to the data and choose Save. Life Form updates the food in the database using the information you've entered.

5. From the Edit Food dialog box, choose Close.

Deleting a Food

You can delete a basic food or recipe from the database using the Delete Food feature. Though you may want to delete a food or recipe you created, we do not advise that you delete any of the foods from the original database. Although the database contains over 13,000 records, deleting individual items will not enhance the performance of the smart search or make entering the foods you eat any easier. More importantly, unlike the item and exercise lists stored in the program's other pages, the food database is not individualized. Everyone using your version of Life Form shares the same food database. Therefore, once you delete a food, you delete it not only for yourself, but also for all other users using your version of Life Form. If you decide you want to delete a basic food or recipe, follow these steps:

1.   From the Food menu, select Delete Food. The Delete Food dialog box appears.

The name you enter must match a food name in the database exactly.

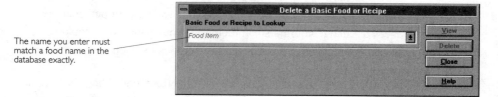

2.   Select the basic food or recipe you want to delete from the drop-down list, and press Tab. Use the same procedure to highlight the food or recipe as described in *Entering a Meal*.

3.   Choose Delete. Life Form displays a warning.

4.   If you are sure you want to delete the food, choose Yes. Life Form then deletes the food or recipe from the food database.

Creating a Recipe from a Meal

If you find that you are entering the same foods in the same amounts time and time again, it is probably because you eat the same meals from week to week. Many of us eat the same combinations of foods in the same amounts both at home and at our favorite restaurants. For example, your standard fast food meal might be a double cheeseburger, a large order of fries, and a medium soda. To save time in entering foods in the Meal Entry Form, you can create recipes from your standard meals. This way you can call up a single item, such as *McDonald's Lunch*, from the database rather than four or five, such as Big Mac, French Fries, Coca-Cola, and Apple Pie. To create a recipe from a meal, follow these steps:

1.   Enter the meal you want to save in the Meal Entry Form, but do not save it. If you have saved the meal previously, you can copy it to the Meal Entry Form from the Meal History by selecting it and clicking on the Copy to Meal button.

2.   After you have entered the last food item in the meal, choose New Recipe from Meal from the Food menu. The Recipe Card dialog box appears.

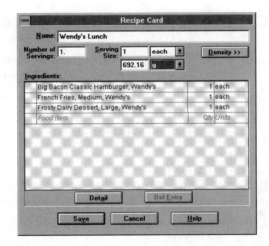

3.   Enter a name for the recipe not to exceed 80 characters.

4.   If you want to change the number of servings or serving size, make the changes in the appropriate boxes. Life Form assumes the entire meal constitutes 1 serving. It also assumes that you will enter the food in the Meal Entry Form using *serving* or *each* as the serving unit. If you plan on entering the food using any other units, you should enter the serving size using those units.

5.   If you want to assign a density, click on the Density button and make a selection from the list or enter a number in the

Density text box. You probably won't want to do this because it is difficult to estimate the collective density of a group of foods.

6. Choose Save. Life Form creates a recipe under the name you have provided and adds it to the food database.

Setting Daily Nutrition Goals

Life Form displays Nutrition Facts on the Food page based on a 2000-calorie diet for women and a 2500-calorie diet for men. These values represent averages and may not be accurate for you. Life Form calculates an alternate daily calorie value based on your height, weight, sex, and Activity Level, which you can use instead of the assigned average value. This alternate value is an estimate of the number of calories you burn each day, so if you are maintaining your current weight, it is also a fair estimate of the number of calories you consume each day. The program also calculates values for fat, saturated fat, cholesterol, sodium, total carbohydrates, and dietary fiber that correspond to this customized calorie value. (For more information on how these values are calculated, see *Daily Reference Values* in the *Notes* section of this chapter.) You can instruct Life Form to use these alternate values by using the Daily Nutrition Goals feature.

✍ *See the Exercise page for an estimate of the number of calories you burn each day.*

You can also use the Daily Nutrition Goals feature to assign your own calorie and nutrient values. You might want to do this if you have a better estimate of how much you eat daily, or if you are dieting and have set goals for the amount of calories or nutrients you want to consume.

To edit Daily Nutrition Goals, follow these steps:

1. From the Food menu, select Daily Nutrition Goals. Life Form displays the Daily Nutrition Goals dialog box.

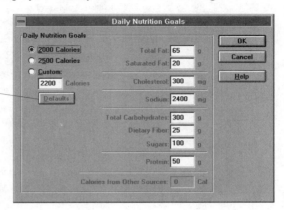

The Defaults Button restores the calculated custom values if you've changed them.

2. Choose one of the three calorie options by clicking on the appropriate radio button. If you choose Custom and want to use Life Form's calculated alternate values, skip to Step 5. If you choose Custom and want to enter your own values, press Tab.

3. If you want to change the number of calories, type an alternate calorie value in the Calorie text box, and press Tab. Life Form calculates values for the listed nutrients based on the calorie value you enter.

4. If you want to edit any of the nutrient values, enter your changes in the appropriate text boxes.

5. Choose OK to apply the new values. Life Form now displays nutrition information based on the values you have entered.

Understanding Calorie Counts

The number of calories in your diet is determined by your intake of energy-producing nutrients, namely fats, carbohydrates, and proteins. Each of these nutrients can be broken down by the body and either used immediately as energy or stored for future use in the form of body fat. The total potential energy these nutrients offer your body is measured in terms of calories. One gram of fat contains 9 calories, or in other words, 9 units of potential energy. One gram of protein and one gram of carbohydrate each contain 4 calories, or 4 units of potential energy. The number of calories a food contains is the sum of calories from fat, carbohydrate, and protein. If, for example, a cookie contains 2 grams of fat, 7 grams of carbohydrate, and 1 gram of protein, its total calorie count is 50. This is the sum of calories from fat (9x2=18), calories from carbohydrate (4x7=28), and calories from protein (4x1=4).

Calories from Other Sources

When Life Form calculates custom calorie and nutrient values, it uses the formula published by the USDA based on height, weight, and other factors. When you enter a new custom value for calories, the nutrient values are recomputed, again using the USDA formula. Sometimes the custom calories and the sum of calories from fat, carbohydrate, and protein aren't equal. The difference appears in the Calories from Other Sources box. A positive number means the number you entered in the Custom Calories text box is greater than the sum. A negative number means the number you entered is less than the sum.

If you edit any of the nutrient values, Life Form uses Calories from

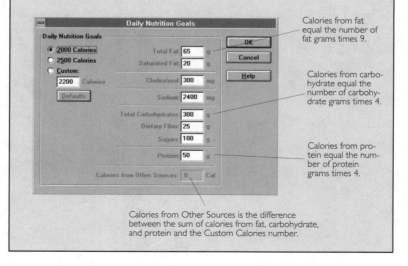

Calories from fat equal the number of fat grams times 9.

Calories from carbohydrate equal the number of carbohydrate grams times 4.

Calories from protein equal the number of protein grams times 4.

Calories from Other Sources is the difference between the sum of calories from fat, carbohydrate, and protein and the Custom Calories number.

Other Sources as an adjustment figure. If, for example, you change the number of total fat grams from 73 to 70, you are subtracting 27 calories, (3 fat grams x 9 calories per fat gram) for the sum of nutrient calories. The program then adds 27 calories to Calories from Other Sources to account for this difference. Because these calories are not linked to any of the nutrients, the percent daily values Life Form calculates might be inaccurate. To eliminate this problem, you can adjust the total fat, total carbohydrates, and protein values until the number of Calories from Other Sources approaches zero.

Calories from Alcohol

If you enter a food or drink containing alcohol in the Meal Entry Form, you might be surprised when you see its nutrition information. If, for example, you entered 1 oz of Rum, you would see this:

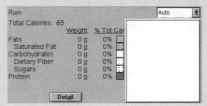

Apparently, the rum contains 65 calories, but none of them come from fats, carbohydrates, or protein. If you viewed the Nutrition Facts for Rum, you'd find the source of these calories.

Alcohol can also be used by the body as energy and therefore is measured in calories. There are 7 calories in each gram of alcohol, but some of these calories might be eliminated from the body before it uses or stores them. Alcohol is not a standard item on the Nutrition Facts label, and for this reason we haven't included it in Daily Nutrition Goals or the display of general nutrition information. *Calories from Alcohol* does appear however in the Nutrition Facts for foods and drinks containing alcohol. If you want to track calories from alcohol, you can include the Calories from Alcohol item in a graph or report on the Graphs page.

Suggestions for Use

Choosing a Strategy for Entering Foods

A number of recent medical studies indicate that many Americans underestimate the number of calories they consume daily, some by as many as 1000 calories. For most of us this inaccuracy results not from indifference or wishful thinking, but from our lack of familiarity with standard weights, measures, and serving sizes. When working with the Food page, the more consistent and accurate you become in entering your foods and their serving sizes, the more accurate Life Form's representation of your diet will be.

The degree of accuracy you seek in keeping your personal record is up to you. If you do not wish to be overly meticulous in your estimations, Life Form makes it easy to achieve a reasonable level of accuracy without much effort. Each basic food and recipe included in the database contains nutrition information based on a standard *serving* size. The program also calculates values for *small servings* and *large servings*, which represent a basic percentage decrease and increase in the standard serving size. By selecting one of these three options depending on your personal eating habits, your estimates will probably be close to the amounts you actually eat. For foods that can be measured in *eaches*, such as cookies, fruits, chips, and candies, you can be fairly accurate by entering the number of items you consume. For example, if you had 2 bananas and 3 cookies for a snack, you can enter these values as eaches and get highly precise data from Life Form regarding their nutrition information.

If you want to be more precise in your estimations than servings and eaches allow, there are a few steps you can take to better your estimating skills. You can begin by familiarizing yourself with basic volume and weight measurements. If you can learn to estimate your food portions in terms of cups or ounces, you might improve the accuracy of your data. There are a few valuable guidelines you can use toward this end. Try using the following examples to become more accurate in your approximations:

Weight	Food
1 g	M & M
3 g	Saltine Cracker
5 g	Grape
1 oz	Strawberry
1.5 oz	Hard Roll
2 oz	Head of Garlic
2.5 oz	Glazed Donut or Lime
5 oz	Lemon
7 oz	Banana or Medium Onion
8 oz	Apple
9 oz	Orange

Volume	Item
1 tsp	Large Grape
1 tbsp	Cherry Tomato
1/3 cup	Lime
2/3 cup	Lemon
1 cup	Large Apple
1 1/2 cup	Large Orange
1 fl oz	Shot Glass
6 fl oz	Juice Glass
12 fl oz	Can of Soda
1 qt	32-fl oz Drink

If you want to go beyond these simple techniques and reach a higher level of precision in estimating your portions, you can take a few steps to educate yourself and sharpen your estimating skills. The best place to begin is your kitchen. With the aid of measuring cups, spoons, and a small scale, you can easily determine your usual serving sizes. Use measuring cups to learn how many fluid ounces your favorite glass holds or how many cups of cereal you pour into your bowl every morning. Use tablespoons and teaspoons to find out how much butter you put on your toast or how much salt you add to your pasta. Weigh the individual foods on your plate to get an idea of how much you normally eat. Once you have weighed and measured for a few days, you can start making guesses and using your tools to check your progress. When you feel comfortable estimating portions of the foods you eat at home, use the skills you've gained to judge how much you eat in restaurants.

Finally, one of the most important steps toward achieving precision in the record you keep is remembering to enter all the foods you eat, rather than most or only a few. Many people forget to include bedtime snacks or mid-morning doughnut breaks when tracking their calorie intake. Omissions can be a significant source of inaccuracy in your food record, so if you are striving for precision, make a serious effort to include everything you eat in your Life Form Meal History.

Understanding Density

Density, though a tricky concept, can be very important to the accuracy of your food entries. It is defined as the mass of a substance per unit volume, and is represented by this formula:

$$Density = Mass / Volume$$

This probably doesn't mean much to you, however, unless you're currently studying chemistry. The easiest way to understand density is to visualize an example, such as this: imagine ten 1-cup measuring cups standing in a line on a table. Each one is filled with a different food or drink. The one on the left end contains popcorn. One toward the middle contains water. The one on the right end contains honey. Each cup represents one cup of the food or drink it contains. Though each cup contains the same volume (1 cup), their contents do not weigh the same. The popcorn weighs 8 grams, the water weighs 118 grams, and the honey weighs 336 grams.

Density is the factor that accounts for these differences. The heavier the food, the greater its density. Density also provides the link we need between volume and weight to determine one in the absence of the other. In other words, if you know an object's weight and approximate density, you can estimate its volume. Likewise, if you know its volume and density, you can calculate its approximate weight.

You may be thinking to yourself, "That's great, but what difference does density make to me?" The answer is maybe none, but maybe quite a bit. The potential problem arises when you go to enter the serving size for a food in cups (a volume measurement) but have added it to the database using ounces (a weight measurement) as the serving size unit. Life Form can convert the serving size in cups to a serving size in ounces using density. If you don't estimate a density, Life Form uses .68 when making conversions. (This is the median density of the foods we've included in the database.) Though for some foods this may be close to the actual density, for many it is not.

Consider the example of tortilla chips. You add a tortilla chip recipe with a serving size as 1 oz, but you do not choose a density. The next time you eat the chips, you estimate that you had about 2 handfuls, or roughly 2 cups. When you enter 2 cups in the Meal Entry Form, your jaw drops in amazement. The program tells you have just consumed 2500 calories. Obviously, this number is not accurate, but it is the best Life Form can do without a density estimate from you. If you want to avoid this problem, estimate a density for each new recipe you add to the database. You can use the examples provided in this list to make your estimate.

Food	Density
Popcorn, Popped	0.05
Corn Flakes	0.1
Tortilla Chips	0.15
Bread, Green Salad	0.25
Bagel	0.3
Peas, Corn, Flour	0.5
Peanuts, Roasted	0.6
Ground Beef, Raw	0.65
Lasagna	0.75
White Rice, Cooked	0.8
Macaroni & Cheese	0.9
Water, Potato Salad	1.0
Pudding	1.3
Honey	1.4

If you don't feel you can estimate a density using these examples, you can perform a simple test to arrive at a more accurate number. Use a food scale to weigh a 1-cup measuring cup in ounces. Then fill the cup with the food you are adding to the database, and weigh it again. Subtract the weight of the measuring cup from the total weight to determine the weight of the food. Divide the weight by 8 (the number of fluid ounces in 1 cup) and use the result as your density. If, for example, you wanted to add potato chips, you might determine that 1 cup of chips weighs 1 ounce. You would then divide 1 by 8 and arrive at a density of .125. What you have done, perhaps without knowing it,

✐ If you're striving for a higher level of accuracy, divide the food's weight in grams by its volume in milliliters.

is measure both the weight and volume of the food and calculate its density using the density formula. The weight you determine using the scale represents mass as measured in ounces, and because there are 8 fluid ounces in 1 cup, the number 8 represents volume as measured in fluid ounces.

*Note: We've assigned a density to all basic foods and recipes in the database. Just as yours will be, our numbers are estimates. If you feel you have a better estimate for a recipe, you can edit the assigned value as described in **Editing a Food**.*

Watching Your Weight

If you have struggled with your weight, you already know how difficult it is to get down to your ideal weight and stay there. The body is an incredible machine, able to adapt to almost any type of food, climate, or situation. It comes with a built-in genetic plan for its size and shape, which seems to change for the bigger as we get older. At times it seems the body perversely opposes any plans we might have to improve it.

There is, of course, no shortage of weight-loss advice from friends, family members, books, infomercials, newspapers, and even tactless strangers. Much of the advice is conflicting (which is better, margarine or butter?), and some of it is downright laughable. Probably the most ridiculous claim is that overweight people would not be overweight if they had not gone on a diet in the first place. In spite of all the advice to the contrary, there doesn't seem to be a magic formula for weight control that works for everyone. Fighting age, genetics, gravity, and inertia (bodies at rest tend to stay at rest) isn't easy. Progress usually comes only with diligent effort.

Unfortunately, Life Form has no magic answer either. It can, however, help you keep track of your efforts more easily. If, for example, your weight loss plan requires you to keep a food log, Life Form's Food page makes it easy to enter foods and see nutrition information. You can also track your weight, waistline, blood pressure, cholesterol, exercise, appetite, and the way you feel each day on the program's other pages. By carefully monitoring the results of your weight loss decisions, you can better understand what helps you and what does not. Hopefully, the information you enter and view with Life Form will motivate you to continue your exercise and dieting efforts long enough to see positive results.

The first step in any weight loss program should be a visit with your doctor. As you make decisions regarding changes to your lifestyle, you should make sure you won't be jeopardizing your health. Before you visit your health professional, you might want to use Life Form to keep track of your regular diet and exercise for a week or two. This will give you a baseline of good information from which to start.

Your next step will probably be to decide on a weight loss strategy. There are, of course, many to choose from. We've described a few of them below and provided suggestions as to how Life Form can help you follow them.

Start an Exercise Program

Of all the different strategies for losing weight, the least controversial and most universally accepted is exercise. While there are disagreements as to the benefits of aerobic over anaerobic, intense versus moderate, and short versus long workouts, practically every health professional agrees that exercise is beneficial.

Not only do you burn calories while exercising, but you also seem to increase your metabolism. Some writers go so far as to say the body automatically adjusts its weight level downward when you participate in a regular exercise program. In addition to promoting weight loss, exercise also improves your health.

You can set a goal for an exercise program with Life Form by following these steps:

1.   From the Exercise page, click on the Lifestyle button located in the Daily Metabolism Estimate group box. The Activity Level Setup dialog box appears.

2.   Enter your Exercise Goal in terms of hours in the Weekly Exercise Activity group box. (Examples of *light* exercises are golf, bowling, and average walking. *Medium* exercises include fast walking, badminton, and dancing. Examples of *intense* exercises are running, aerobics, and cross country skiing.)

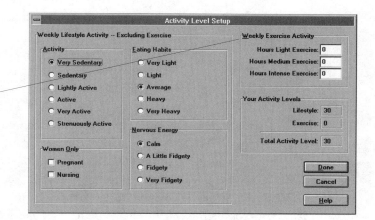

You can use the Weekly Exercise Activity group box to set an Exercise Goal.

3.   After you enter your goal, choose Done to close the Activity Level Setup dialog box. Life Form returns to the Exercise page.

Life Form approximates the number of calories you burn from exercise over the course of a day and a week using the numbers you provide in the Activity Level Setup. These figures appear in the Exercise Calories group box in the row labeled *Estimated (from Activity Level)*. The program also calculates the actual number of calories you burn from exercise based on the entries you make in the Exercise Journal. The actual and estimated values are shown next to each other, so you can check to see how closely the calories from your goal match the calories from your actual exercise.

You can also compare your exercise goal to your actual exercise by creating an exercise graph. To create an exercise graph, see *Creating an Exercise Graph* in the *Suggestions for Use* section of *Chapter 9, Graphs*.

Count Food Calories

This method has largely gone out of favor, but might work for some people. The basic idea is simple enough: since a pound of fat contains about 3500 calories, you should lose a pound for every 3500 calories you don't eat. If, for example, your body requires 2500 calories a day to maintain its current weight, then eating 2000 calories a day for a week should produce a one-pound weight loss.

Of course, the body is not that simple. It can adapt to a lower caloric intake by lowering its metabolism, perhaps enough to erase any benefit of the reduction in calories. Some people fail to lose weight on diets of less than 1000 calories per day because their metabolism slows so drastically. With very-low-calorie diets, the body may burn muscle instead of fat, even to the point of damaging internal organs. (Although we hesitate to give advice, we strongly suggest you never try a very-low-calorie diet.) Although we can't make any guarantees, if you can keep your metabolism up while limiting your intake of calories, you should be able to lose weight.

If you decide to count calories, you can monitor your progress by setting a Daily Calorie Goal. (See *Setting Daily Nutrition Goals* in this chapter for instructions on setting a Daily Calorie Goal.) Once you have set your Daily Calorie Goal, Life Form shows you nutrition information based on the goal. If, for example, you set a goal of 2100 calories, the Nutrition Facts and general nutrition information for each food you enter will be represented as a percentage of a 2100-calorie diet.

You can monitor your progress in counting calories by creating a Calorie Goal graph comparing your calories consumed to your daily calories goal. A Calories graph comparing calories consumed (as calculated on the Food page) to calories burned (as calculated on the Exercise page) can also be helpful in monitoring your overall dieting success. To create a Calorie Goal graph or to use the predefined Calories graph, see the *Suggestions for Use* section of *Chapter 9, Graphs*.

If you decide to count calories, you have to remember that the metabolism estimates on the Exercise page are made for the average person. Over time you might find that you are not losing weight even though the program indicates you should be. If this is the case, you can adjust your Activity Level downward so that your metabolism estimate for calories burned matches your calories consumed. Then you can try lowering your calorie intake still further to see if the change affects your weight. As with any diet, please consult your doctor to make sure it is safe.

Limit Fat

Dietary guidelines published by the US Government encourage us to reduce our fat intake to less than 30% of total daily calories. Some diet programs go so far as to limit fat to 10-20% of total calories. While there are many who believe dietary fat is the primary culprit in obesity, not all research bears this out. Over the past few years Americans have reduced their fat intake a little, but their weight has gone up. The reason for the increase may be that we are replacing fat with sugar. 44-fluid ounce Bladder Busters (soft drinks from convenience stores) could be more of a problem in the average American diet than fat. If you decide to limit your fat intake, you might want to keep a close eye on your sugar intake.

If you are monitoring your fat intake, you can use Life Form to track your progress. To do this, you should first set a Fat Goal on the Food page by following these steps:

1.   From the Food menu on the Food page, select Daily Nutrition Goals. The Daily Nutrition Goals dialog box appears.

Set your goals for Total Fat and Saturated Fat in these text boxes.

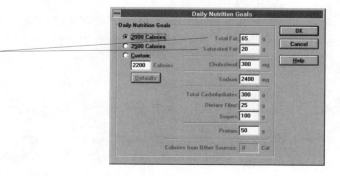

2.   Click on the Custom radio button, then press Tab.

3.   If you haven't already entered a Calorie Goal, enter one in the Calories text box or press Tab to select Life Form's calculated custom calorie value.

✎ Be sure your Fat Goal exceeds your Saturated Fat goal.

4.   Enter your Fat Goal in the Total Fat text box. If you have a Saturated Fat Goal, enter it in the Saturated Fat text box.

5.   Choose OK.

You can monitor your progress in limiting fat intake by creating a Dietary Fat graph comparing your actual fat intake to your fat goal, or a Saturated Fat graph comparing your actual saturated fat intake to your Saturated Fat Goal. To create a Dietary Fat or Saturated Fat graph, see *Tracking a Special Diet with a Graph* in the *Suggestions for Use* section of *Chapter 9, Graphs*.

Limit Carbohydrates

Low-carbohydrate diets are a popular yet controversial dieting alternative. Promoters of these plans encourage dieters to replace a percentage of their carbohydrate calories with protein and fat calories. This promotes ketosis, a process by which fats in the blood are metabolized and expelled from the body. Though critics believe low-carbohydrate programs can lead to physical complications, advocates claim them to be a safe and effective means of weight loss.

If you want to monitor your carbohydrate intake, you can set a Total Carbohydrate Goal in the Daily Nutrition Goals dialog box and create a Carbohydrate graph on the Graphs page. To create a Carbohydrate graph, see *Tracking a Special Diet with a Graph* in the *Suggestions for Use* section of *Chapter 9, Graphs*.

Switch from Refined to Complex Carbohydrates

Eliminating sugar, white flour, white rice, chips, and other sources of "empty calories" from the diet is thought by some to be an advantage in weight control. There is evidence to suggest that digestion of refined carbohydrates can produce an unnecessarily high level of insulin in the bloodstream. The high insulin level is thought to encourage weight gain, as well as cause other problems, such as headaches, indigestion, and perhaps hardening of the arteries. Vegetables, whole fruits (fruit juice has a lot of sugar), and whole grains seem to be digested with a reasonable level of insulin, and are thought to provide numerous health benefits.

Life Form does not have categories for complex and refined carbohydrates. Instead, the categories match the Nutrition Facts label, with carbohydrates divided into sugar, fiber, and total. You will, however, see your fiber percentage go up and your sugar percentage go down as you eat more complex carbohydrates. You can monitor your fiber and sugar intake by setting fiber and sugar goals on the Food page and creating goal graphs on the Graphs page.

Switch to a Vegetarian Diet

Some say, "I've never met a fat vegetarian." While not for everyone, vegetarianism can be an effective way to lose weight. Life Form does not make a distinction between animal and other types of protein, because its nutrition information matches the Nutrition Facts label. You can, however, graph the start of a vegetarian diet by entering it as an event on the History page, and marking the event to be graphed. (Add it as an Other type event.) This event will then appear on your graphs, so you can see your weight progress from that date, and any other ratings, measurements, or chemistry items that are important to you.

Try a Supplement

While we are not aware of a magic pill that always leads to weight loss, there are some people who claim to have good results using health food store supplements. Some of the supplements include stimulants such as caffeine or guarana, which may have undesirable side effects. If you decide to use a supplement, be careful to closely monitor your results.

Use a Commercial Weight-Loss Center

Businesses like Weight Watchers, Jenny Craig, Diet Center, and

Nutri/System can provide additional help and motivation, however, this attention comes with a price. Most of the commercial centers require you to keep a food log, a task that Life Form makes much easier. By setting goals and graphing results, you can easily adapt Life Form to the strategy promoted by the center you choose.

This list of strategies is by no means exhaustive. You will, no doubt, find many other strategies as you try to lose weight. If you keep track of your health information as you try different things, Life Form can help you understand what works for you and what does not.

Tracking Food Intolerances, Sensitivities, and Allergies

Many of us go through life suffering regular headaches, skin irritations, congestion, and other symptoms without knowing they may be a direct result of the foods we eat. Whether the symptoms are merely an annoyance or so severe they prevent us from functioning, they can often be reduced or eliminated by changing our diets. Life Form can help you detect food intolerances, sensitivities, and allergies. Simply monitor symptoms using the Ratings page and the foods you eat using the Food page. You can then create a graph showing the dates of occurrence and/or severity of your symptoms and compare it to your Meal History. If you discover that you consistently suffer from headaches after eating meals containing shellfish, you might want to eliminate shellfish from your diet.

Of course, there is a chance that shellfish are not the cause of your headaches. After omitting a suspicious food from your diet, you should continue to monitor your symptoms to determine whether the change is effective in eliminating them.

Menu Planning

While Life Form is a valuable tool in tracking the foods you eat after you eat them, you can also use it as an aid in menu planning. By reviewing the nutrition content of foods before you prepare them, you can decide what foods best fit within your individual dietary guidelines. If, for example, you are trying to limit your saturated fat grams to 30 per day and want to prepare a tuna casserole for dinner, you can call up the nutrition information for *Tuna Casserole* to see if it meets your criteria.

You can also use Life Form to make immediate decisions regarding what you do and don't eat. If at the end of the day you want to eat a piece of pie, but aren't sure if you've already exceeded your daily calorie allowance, you can check your food calories for the day by selecting *Today* from the list of display options. You may decide you should pass on the pie, since you've already consumed more than the number of calories your diet prescribes.

Notes

The Nutrition Facts Label

For years consumers have been confounded and confused by the little numbers that appear on food nutrition information labels. Typically, labels have offered a lot of information, but little context for understanding it. Questions such as, "Just what does nine grams of fat mean to me?" and "Is riboflavin really important?" have not been uncommon among curious shoppers. Concerned by the inadequacy and inconsistency of food labels, the FDA recently developed a new food label. The label, commonly known by the name Nutrition Facts, is designed to increase accuracy and help consumers make more informed decisions about the foods they eat.

The basis of the Nutrition Facts label is a new set of dietary components, reflected both by weight and as a percentage of daily nutritional needs. Manufacturers must now list values for the following items: total calories, calories from fat, total fat, saturated fat, cholesterol, sodium, total carbohydrate, dietary fiber, sugars, protein, vitamin A, vitamin C, calcium, and iron. The FDA selected the nutrients in this group based on their public health significance and current government dietary recommendations, namely the belief that less fat and more fiber in the average American's diet is beneficial.

By referring to the % Daily Value column of the new label, consumers can determine how individual foods fit into their overall diets. The percentages provided are based on a 2,000 calorie diet and reflect the government's recommendations for limiting fat, cholesterol, and sodium intake. Some labels may provide additional values based on a 2,500 calorie diet if space allows. Life Form calculates values for both the 2,000 and 2,500 calorie standards and also gives you the option of assigning a calorie level to reflect your personal diet. When the program displays nutrition data, it bases it on the calorie level you choose.

Whereas manufacturers set the serving sizes listed on old nutrition labels, the FDA now determines standard serving sizes for foods by category. This prevents manufacturers from manipulating data to their advantage and makes it easier for consumers to compare data between brands. Serving sizes are provided in both metric and common household units so consumers can better understand just what constitutes a serving.

Reference Daily Intakes (RDIs)*

You might be familiar with Reference Daily Intakes (RDIs) because they used to be known as U.S. Recommended Daily Allowances (U.S. RDAs). The Food and Drug Administration (FDA) has calculated the following RDIs based on 2,000 calories per day for adults and children over 4.

Nutrient	Amount
Vitamin A	5,000 International Units (IU)
Vitamin C	60 mg
Calcium	1.0 g
Iron	18 mg

*Based on National Academy of Sciences' 1968 Recommended Dietary Allowances

Daily Reference Values (DRVs)

The FDA has assigned Daily Reference Values (DRVs) for nutrients not previously covered by U.S. RDAs. Like the RDIs, most of the DRVs are based on a 2,000-calorie diet. The values for cholesterol, sodium, and potassium are the same for adults and children over 4, regardless of caloric intake.

Food Component	DRV	Based on...
Fat	65 g	30% of total calories
Saturated Fatty Acids	20 g	10% of total calories
Cholesterol	300 mg	
Total Carbohydrate	300 g	60% of total calories
Fiber	25 g	11.5 g per 1,000 calories
Sodium	2,400 mg	
Potassium	3,500 mg	
Protein	50 g*	10% of calories

*DRV for protein does not apply to certain populations; Reference Daily Intake (RDI) has been established for these groups: children 1 to 4 years: 16g; infants under 1 year: 14 g; pregnant women: 60 g; nursing mothers: 65 g.

(Source for RDI/DRV information: FDA Consumer, Focus on Food Labeling, May 1993.)

Abbreviations for Serving Size Units

Abbreviation	Unit
oz	ounce
lb	pound
floz	fluid ounce
tsp	teaspoon
tbsp	tablespoon
pt	pint
qt	quart
gal	gallon
cu in	cubic inch
srv	serving
srv, sm	small serving
srv, lrg	large serving
ea, sm	small each
ea, lrg	large each
mg	milligram
g	gram
kg	kilogram
cc	cubic centimeter
ml	milliliter
l	liter

The Life Form Food Database

Database Methodology

The Life Form food database comprises nutrition information for over 13,000 foods, including fresh, processed, prepared, and restaurant foods. The data was collected from the USDA, manufacturer Nutrition Facts labels, published food content guides, food manufacturers and restaurant chains. Each food record contains values for the categories and nutrients specified on the new nutrition label: serving size, calories, calories from fat, total fat, saturated fat, cholesterol, sodium, total carbohydrate, dietary fiber, sugars, protein, vitamin A, vitamin C, calcium, and iron. Although some of you may be interested in tracking other food nutrients and ingredients such as caffeine, aspartame, and riboflavin, in an attempt to maintain accuracy, we have included only those nutrients listed on the new label. Because food manufacturers are not required to provide figures for such categories, we have no way of accurately estimating their presence in foods, nor would you have an accurate way of including them in the foods and recipes you add to the food database.

Values for approximately 4,000 raw and generic processed foods were taken from the United States Department of Agriculture's Nutrient Data Base for Standard Reference. The USDA began evaluating the composition of foods in 1950, when it published Agriculture Handbook No. 8, and has continued to add and update nutrition information ever since. The USDA provides values for sugar content of around 1,000 foods separately under the title of the Home Economic Research Report.

Data for over 5,500 processed name brand foods was gathered from Nutrition Facts labels published on food packages and also from literature circulated by various food manufacturers. We collected information from national and regional restaurant chains on their prepared foods, adding over 1,000 additional foods to the database. Recipes of commonly and some uncommonly prepared foods account for an additional 1,500 entries.

In entering your meals, you may find that despite the breadth of the Life Form database, some of the foods you eat are not included. There are many possible explanations for their absence. First, roughly 10% of processed foods are not required to bear the Nutrition Facts label. Foods prepared by small businesses, prepared on site, or containing little to no nutritional value are exempt from the current regulations. Suppliers of raw foods are also free from labeling requirements; however, the USDA's database contains values for a majority of fruits, vegetables, and meats. Restaurants are not required to publish nutrition information for their foods, although in an effort to win the confidence of consumers, many chains and franchises do. Most of these chains agreed to let us publish their data, while a small percentage refused. If your favorite establishment's foods are not included in the database, it is likely they either denied us permission to use their information or do not publish it at all.

While the database is extensive and contains complete information for most foods, you should be aware that the accuracy of this information is subject to certain limitations. The USDA provides nutritional values for fresh and generic brand foods, which are commonly accepted as the standard within the food industry. The government does not, however, guarantee its data to be 100% or even 90% accurate. Similarly, in regulating manufacturers of prepared foods, the Food and Drug Administration (FDA) allows for a 20% margin of error. Locally prepared and regionally distributed products are not as closely regulated as national ones and may exceed the 20% rule. Data circulated by restaurants is not subject to FDA regulations, and its accuracy is therefore uncertain.

Many restaurant foods and foods contained in the USDA database did not offer values for sugar. To present a complete picture of these foods, we have estimated their sugar content based on values for similar foods. When a sugar value was missing from a food record, our nutrition team found a similar food and divided its total carbohydrate grams by its sugar content to arrive at a carbohydrate to sugar ratio. This ratio was then used to calculate an approximate sugar value for the incomplete food record. Whenever possible, food records containing approximated information were replaced with complete data from other sources such as privately published food count books and updated Nutrition Facts labels.

This same technique was used in approximating fiber, vitamin, and mineral values for many of the fast food entries. The fast food data provided by restaurants was about 50% complete, while the other 50% ranged from missing one item to missing vitamins, minerals, sugar, and fiber. In cases of incomplete data, we approximated values by calculating the ratio of the nutrient to total weight for a similar food and applying the ratio to the incomplete record. If, for example, Pizza Hut did not provide vitamin C values, we took the ratio of vitamin C to total weight for a similar Domino's entry and applied it to the Pizza Hut record. In some instances, however, there were no similar foods to use in this way. In these cases we created a recipe using Life Form and applied the calculated values to the food record. Denny's Denver Omelet, for example, did not come with a portion of the needed data. To gather this data we created a recipe for a standard one serving omelet, checked the resulting data against that provided by Denny's, and filled in the missing data.

Despite these limitations, you should feel confident that by using Life Form you will get a good overall picture of your diet and its nutrient breakdown. Life Form provides you with the most up-to-date information available, as well as an accurate means of entering nutrient values for new foods and calculating values for recipe foods. You should be aware, however, that in nutrition, the greatest element of error does not arise from incomplete or rounded data, but rather from miscalculations of food size or quantity. Please refer to *Choosing a Strategy for Entering Foods* in the *Suggestions for Use* section of this chapter for suggestions on achieving accuracy and consistency in entering the foods you eat in the Life Form database.

Food Naming Conventions

Achieving consistency in the naming of Life Form's food database records seems a virtual impossibility, even when a strict set of rules is applied. Exceptions are numerous and information often becomes confusing if presented in a single format for all types and varieties of foods. The presiding rule, therefore, is to present all information in a way that is easy to read, while choosing the specific format that seems most logical for each food type. Although these slight variations in form are virtually transparent to users, by mirroring their expectations and entry patterns, we hope to maximize the speed and accuracy of Life Form's smart search.

The rules that apply to all records are as follows:

1.   Information is separated by commas.

2.   The first letter of all words is capitalized (including words linked by hyphens) except those of conjunctions and prepositions.

3.   No abbreviations or symbols are used except "&".

The basic rules governing non-brand-name foods are as follows:

1. Food name is presented first including variety modifiers that would likely be included when describing the product, e.g., "I had vanilla ice cream, lemon meringue pie, or iceberg lettuce." (Note: Claims with regard to fat or sugar content are not included before the food name, with the exception of diet sodas, e.g., Diet Coke, Diet 7Up. They are considered other modifiers as defined below.)

2. Other modifiers that would not normally be used when describing the product follow the food name, e.g., Peaches, Sweetened; Chicken without Skin; Cottage Cheese, Lowfat. (Note: If the modifier can be characterized by a prepositional phrase, no comma is inserted.)

3. Manner of packaging follows the other modifiers, e.g., Green Beans, Canned; French Fries, Frozen. Manner of packaging is not included for foods packaged in only one way, e.g., Tortilla Chips rather than Tortilla Chips, Bagged; and Corn Flakes Cereal rather than Corn Flakes Cereal, Boxed.

4. Manner of preparation is the last piece of information listed in a non-brand-name food, e.g., Green Beans, Canned, Boiled; French Fries, Frozen, Oven-Heated. There is a major exception to this rule for foods commonly described by their manner of preparation, e.g., Fried Chicken, Scrambled Eggs, Stewed Tomatoes.

When brand names are added to records, the rules become slightly more complicated. Many products are known by their brand names, e.g., Doritos, Kool-Aid, Equal, Oreos, Pepsi, Rice Krispies. Other products are commonly associated with their manufacturer, but not identified as such, e.g., corn packaged by Green Giant or potatoes prepared and packaged by Ore-Ida.

Given these conditions, we have formulated the following rules with regard to brand-name products:

1. If the brand name is also a common name by which the product is known, it is placed first in the record, followed by the food name with preceding and following modifiers, e.g., Doritos Cool Ranch Tortilla Chips, Kool-Aid Purplesaurus Rex Fruit Drink.

2. A food name should be assigned to all foods, even those commonly know by their brand name only, e.g., Pringle's Potato Crisps, Funyuns Onion-Flavored Rings, Slice Mandarin Orange Soda. (Exceptions: Hamburger Helper, Tuna Helper, Suddenly Salad. The varieties of these foods are sufficiently descriptive to exclude *meal mix* or some other confusing term, e.g., Hamburger Helper Potato Stroganoff.)

3. Manufacturer name is not included in the record if unnecessary to brand name recognition, e.g., Better Cheddars Crackers rather than Better Cheddars Crackers, Nabisco; and Special K Cereal, rather than Special K Cereal, Kellogg's.

4. Manufacturer name is included in record after brand name, if brand name has become a generic term by which other products are known, e.g., Raisin Bran Cereal, Post and Corn Flakes Cereal, Kellogg's.

5. Brand/manufacturer name is listed last in the record if not necessary to product recognition, e.g., Baked Beans, Canned, S&W; Lasagna, Frozen, Stouffer's.

6. Brand name may follow manufacturer name if including it in the food name becomes confusing, e.g., Peanut Butter Granola Bar, Quaker Chewy rather than Chewy Peanut Butter Granola Bar, Quaker.

7. Brand name and manufacturer name are included in fast food entries, e.g., Egg McMuffin, McDonald's; Whopper Hamburger, Burger King.

Sample Records

Applesauce, Sweetened, Canned
Cheddar Cheese, Shredded, Kraft
Peach, Raw
Cool Whip Non-Dairy Topping
Strawberry Toaster Pastry
Tomato and Herb Spaghetti Sauce, Ragu
Fig Newtons Cookies

Cap'n Crunch Peanut Butter Crunch Cereal
Big Classic Hamburger, Wendy's
Chow Mein Noodles with Sesame Bits, Chun King
Bacon-Flavored Crackers, Nabisco
Boysenberries, Canned in Heavy Syrup
Ham, Chopped, Canned
Scrambled Eggs

EXERCISE

For those who exercise regularly, Life Form's Exercise page provides an easy way to record workout information and monitor training programs. The Exercise Journal helps you keep a detailed history of your exercise activity. When you enter exercises in the Journal, Life Form estimates the number of calories you burn. Even if you never enter an exercise, Life Form displays an estimate of your daily calorie expenditure using information you provide in the User Setup.

This chapter explains how to keep an Exercise Journal and monitor calorie expenditures using the Exercise page.

Basic Features

The Exercise page is divided into two sections that make tracking your exercise and calorie expenditures easy. The Exercise Journal is located in the top portion of the screen and lets you record your daily exercise activity by type of exercise, duration, and intensity. Each time you exercise, you can enter this information and Life Form will estimate the number of calories you burn. The Calorie window displays two groups of information: *Exercise Calories* and the *Daily Metabolism Estimate*. Life Form approximates the number of calories you burn from exercise and displays both daily and weekly estimates in the Exercise Calories group box. The program also calculates an estimate of the total number of calories you burn each day based on your exercise and the information you enter in the User Setup. It displays this value in the Daily Metabolism Estimate group box.

EXERCISE

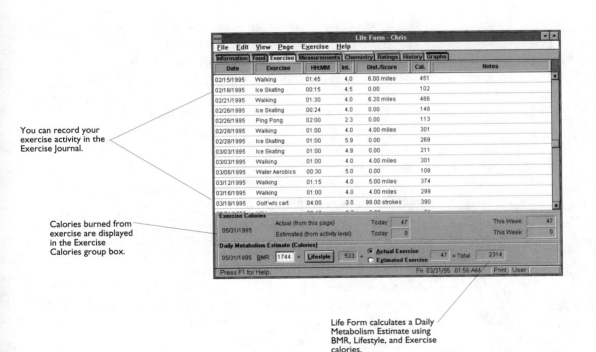

You can record your exercise activity in the Exercise Journal.

Calories burned from exercise are displayed in the Exercise Calories group box.

Life Form calculates a Daily Metabolism Estimate using BMR, Lifestyle, and Exercise calories.

Entering an Exercise Record

When you open the Exercise page, Life Form displays a blank entry at the end of the Exercise Journal and the date field has the focus. You can begin entering your exercises by following these steps:

1. Click on the Date field of the blank record if it does not have the focus.

The month area of the Date field has the focus.

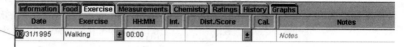

✍See *Entering Times and Dates* in the Notes section of this chapter for tips on entering dates in Life Form.

2. Enter the date you did the exercise, and press Tab. Before, you enter a date, Life Form displays the current date in the date field. If you are entering an exercise for the current date, you may tab to the next field.

3. Choose an exercise from the drop-down list by clicking on it. Then press Tab. (If the exercise you want to enter does not appear in the list, you can add it following the steps listed in *Adding a New Exercise*.)

4. Enter the time you spent doing the exercise in terms of hours and minutes, then press Tab.

    Life Form refers to this value as *duration*. The program needs a duration to calculate calorie expenditures for all exercises except walking and running. If you do not enter a duration, Life Form displays a warning.

5. If you like, edit the intensity for the exercise, then press Tab.

✍See *Estimating Intensity in the Suggestions for Use* section of this chapter for tips on changing intensity.

    Life Form assigns all predefined exercises an intensity. It uses this level to calculate calories burned for your exercise entries. When you choose an exercise from the Exercise list, Life Form displays the intensity for that exercise in the Intensity field. You can replace the predefined intensity value by clicking on the Intensity field and entering a number between 0.1 and 9.9.

See Windows Skill 14 for tips on using list boxes.

6. Enter a distance or score for the exercise, if appropriate, by entering a number and then selecting a unit of measure from the drop-down list box. Then press Tab.

   You are not required to enter a distance for distance-related exercises, such as swimming and cycling, but doing so allows you to track your progress more easily. If you enter a distance for either running or walking, Life Form uses the value in calculating calories for these exercises. You can use score for activities like golf and bowling. Though Life Form does not use score in calorie calculations, you may find it useful in tracking your progress.

7. If you want to change the number of calories burned, enter a different number in the *Calories (Cal.)* field. Then press Tab.

   Life Form calculates the number of calories you burn using the figures you enter for duration and intensity/heart rate. If you have access to data from an alternate source, such as the manufacturer of your personal home gym or workout machine, you can override Life Form's calculation by entering a different number. Before you do this, however, you should be aware of how Life Form calculates exercise calories burned. See *Using Other Sources of Calorie Calculations* in the *Suggestions for Use* section of this chapter for an explanation of the differences between the program's calculations and those provided by equipment manufacturers.

8. If you have any comments or information you want to include, enter them in the Notes field.

   You can use the Notes field to record any information about the exercise. You may want to note how you felt or factors that affected your performance, such as weather. You can also use this field to keep a record of your opponents or partners.

9. Press Enter. Life Form saves the entry into the Exercise Journal.

WINDOWS SKILL 14 — USING LIST BOXES

List boxes display groups of options from which you select one, or in some cases, multiple items. There are a number of ways to choose an item from a single-selection list box. One is to click on the item in the list. Another is to use the up and down arrow keys to move through the list to the desired selection and then press Tab. You can also select an item by typing characters. When you type a letter, a selection from the list that begins with the letter appears. If no selections begin with that letter, the selection that is first in the list or already highlighted appears. You can type the same letter again to move to the item beginning with that letter that is next in the list. This can be a little confusing, because Windows only matches the first letter of a selection. If, for example, you wanted to choose *B Neg* from the blood type list and typed "B," *B Pos* would appear as the selected option. If you then typed "N" because it is the next letter in *B Neg*, the selection would not change. If you typed "B" again, however, the selection would change to *B Neg* because it is the next item in the list beginning with "B."

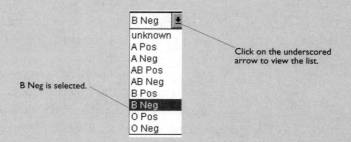

Click on the underscored arrow to view the list.

B Neg is selected.

Most single-selection list boxes in Life Form are drop-down lists boxes like this one. When you click on the arrow box to their immediate right, they open to display possible selections.

Life Form's multiple-selection list boxes display check boxes next to the items in the list. When an item is selected an "X" appears in its check box. When it is not, the check box remains empty. You can select and deselect items in the list by clicking on their check boxes.

An "X" in an item's checkbox means the item is selected.

Items:
- ☒ Fluid Retention
- ☐ Frustration
- ☐ Headache
- ☐ Heartburn
- ☐ Hot Flashes
- ☐ Indecisiveness
- ☐ Indigestion
- ☒ Insomnia
- ☐ Intestinal Gas
- ☐ Irregular Heartbeat
- ☐ Irritability
- ☐ Love Life
- ☐ Menstrual Flow
- ☐ Nausea
- ☒ Nosebleed
- ☐ Numbness

EXERCISE

Inserting an Exercise Record

Life Form stores records in the Exercise Journal according to date. If you are entering a record that belongs between existing records, you can insert it in the Journal in one of two ways. The first is to enter the record at the bottom of the Journal and let Life Form move it to its proper spot once you press Enter. If you prefer to see the record in its correct place as you enter it, you can insert it by following these steps:

1. Click on the record in the Journal that will immediately follow the new record.

✍Or type Ctrl+I.

2. From the Edit menu, choose Insert Entry. Life Form inserts a blank entry before the selected record.

3. Enter information following the steps listed in *Entering an Exercise Record.*

   Note: If you insert a record out of order, Life Form moves it to its proper spot in the Journal.

Editing an Exercise Record

To edit any of the information entered on the Exercise page, click on the field you want to edit, type your changes, and press Enter. Life Form automatically stores the most recent changes without you having to press any additional keys.

Deleting an Exercise Record

To delete an exercise record, follow these steps:

✍Or click on the record and type Ctrl+D.

1.	Click anywhere in the record and click on the Del Entry button on the Status bar. (You can also select Delete Entry from the Edit menu.) The following message appears:

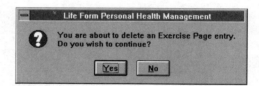

2.	Choose Yes. Life Form deletes the record from the Exercise Journal.

Adding a New Exercise

Life Form's exercise database contains information for 50 exercises. The program tracks data and calculates calorie expenditures for these exercises automatically. If your favorite exercises are not included in the database, you can add them by providing a few basic details. Once you have added an exercise to the database, Life Form can record information and make calculations for that exercise as it does for the predefined ones.

To add a new exercise to the Exercise list, follow these steps:

✍Or choose <new> from the drop-down list of exercises in a record.

1. From the Exercise menu, select New Exercise. The New Exercise dialog box appears.

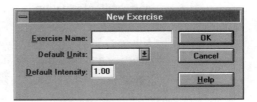

2. Enter an exercise name not to exceed 15 characters. The name may be more than one word.

3. If the exercise you are adding can be measured in sets, strokes, laps, or a distance unit such as miles, choose a unit from the drop-down list box.

✍See List of Exercises in the Notes section of this chapter for examples of different intensities.

4. Enter an intensity for the new exercise between 0.1 and 9.9.

5. Choose OK. The new exercise now appears alphabetically in the Exercise list.

Editing an Exercise

You may want to edit an exercise by changing its name, default units, or default intensity. You can use the Edit Exercise feature to edit both the predefined exercises and those you add to the list. To edit an exercise, follow these steps:

1. From the Exercise menu, select Edit Exercise. The Exercise list dialog box appears.

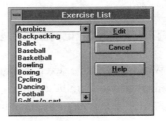

2.   Click on the name of the exercise you want to edit and choose
       Edit. The Edit Exercise dialog box appears.

3.   Change the exercise name, units, or intensity by typing the
       corrected information in the appropriate field.

4.   Choose OK. Life Form updates the database record for the
       exercise and uses the new information to display records and
       calculate data.

Deleting an Exercise

If you want to delete an exercise from the Exercise list, follow these
steps:

1.   From the Exercise menu, select Delete Exercise. The Exercise
       List dialog box appears.

2.   Click on the name of the exercise you want to delete, and then
       choose Delete. Life Form displays a warning.

3.   Choose OK. Life Form deletes the exercise from the Exercise
       list.

If you decide later you want to add a deleted exercise back to the list,
follow the procedure described in *Adding a New Exercise*. Refer to the
List of Exercises located in the *Notes* section of this chapter for distance and intensity values.

Note: You cannot delete Walking, Jogging, or Running from the list.

Tracking Calorie Expenditures

Whether you enter exercises in the Exercise Journal or not, you may be
interested to learn how many calories you burn from day to day. Life
Form displays calorie calculations at the bottom of the Exercise page in

the group boxes labeled *Exercise Calories* and *Daily Metabolism Estimate (Calories)*. The program can calculate calorie expenditures using both your Exercise Journal and the exercise information you enter in the Activity Level Setup. You do not need to record exercises in the Exercise Journal for Life Form to estimate your calories burned from exercise or lifestyle. The information you provided in your User Setup is sufficient for these calculations.

Note: Because metabolism is a complex process that varies from person to person, Life Form's calculations cannot be exact for every individual. While they may be close, you should remember that the numbers you see represent estimates of your calorie expenditure rather than actual values.

Exercise Calories

Life Form totals the number of calories you burn from exercise on both a daily and weekly basis. The Exercise Calories group box, located directly below the Exercise Journal, displays calculations for the *date highlighted in the Journal* and its corresponding week. (Life Form calculates values based on a Sunday to Saturday week.) If no entries have been made in the Journal, Life Form displays calculations for the *current date* and its corresponding week.

Life Form displays calorie estimates for the date currently highlighted in the Exercise Journal.

Exercise Calories					
03/31/1995	Actual (from this page)	Today:	154	This Week:	616
	Estimated (from activity level)	Today:	171	This Week:	342

✍ *You can choose from estimated or actual calories burned when viewing exercise calories.*

If you use the Exercise Journal, Life Form computes the number of calories you have burned based on the exercises you've entered. The program displays values for *Today* and *This Week* in the top row labeled *Actual (from this Page)*. If you do not use the Journal, the actual value will be 0.

The program also calculates an estimated value based on the figures you provided in the Activity Level Setup. You may recall that when you went through the New User Setup, Life Form asked you to estimate the number of hours you spend each week in light, medium, and intense exercise. Using these numbers, Life Form approximates the

✍See the Notes section of this chapter for a detailed explanation of how Life Form makes its calorie calculations.

number of calories you burn from exercise over the course of a day and a week. These figures appear in the row labeled *Estimated (from Activity Level)*. Because Life Form displays the actual and estimated values next to each other, you can check to see how closely the calories from your estimate match the calories from your actual exercise. If your estimate is not as close as you want it to be, you can change it in the Activity Level Setup.

Daily Metabolism Estimate

Below the Exercise Calories group box, Life Form displays another group box labeled *Daily Metabolism Estimate (Calories)*. Here Life Form provides you with an estimate of the number of calories you burn in a given day. As with exercise calories, the program shows information for either the date highlighted in the Exercise Journal or the current date.

✍You can click on the Lifestyle button to view your Activity Level Setup.

The Daily Metabolism Estimate comprises three basic elements: BMR (basal metabolic rate), or the minimum number of calories your body burns to keep functioning; lifestyle calories; and exercise calories. Life Form calculates your BMR and lifestyle calories using the information you provide in the User Setup. (For an explanation of these calculations, see the *Notes* section of this chapter.) You choose whether you want the program to use actual or estimated exercise calories by clicking on one of the two radio buttons provided. The total calorie figure displayed to the far right of the group box is the sum of BMR, lifestyle calories, and exercise calories.

Printing the Exercise Journal

You can print any or all of your Exercise Journal by following these steps :

✎ *Or type Ctrl+P.*

1. Click on the Print button in the Status bar. (You can also select Print from the File menu.) The Print dialog box appears.

2. Specify the date range you want to print by entering dates in the From and To text boxes. If you do not edit the beginning and ending dates, Life Form prints your entire Journal.

3. Choose OK. Life Form prints your selection.

Advanced Features

Using Heart Rate Instead of Intensity

✍ Or select Heart Rate from the Exercise menu.

If you prefer to calculate your exercise calories using heart rate rather than intensity, click on the box labeled *Int.* at the top of the Exercise Journal. The heading *H.R.* replaces *Int.* and a heart rate corresponding to the intensity level appears.

✍ See *Estimating Intensity* in the *Suggestions for Use* section of this chapter for an explanation of the relationship between intensity and heart rate.

You can edit the heart rate for the record by clicking on the appropriate field and entering a new number. If you toggle back to intensity after editing a heart rate, you will notice that Life Form adjusts the intensity level to reflect your change. Similarly, if you change the intensity level for an entry, the program recalculates the corresponding heart rate.

Controlling Warning Dialogs

The program regularly displays a warning if you have not entered sufficient user information in the User Setup to make exercise calorie calculations. If you don't want to see this warning, you can instruct Life Form not to display it. To disable the exercise warning dialog, follow these steps:

1.   From the Exercise menu, choose Options. The Options dialog box appears.

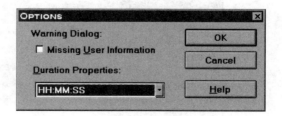

2.   Click on the Missing User Information check box.

3.   Choose OK.

If you decide later that you want Life Form to display the warning, return to the Options dialog and reselect the Missing User Information option.

Changing Duration Properties

✍ Or choose a setting from the Options dialog box.

Life Form assumes you will record duration for your exercise in terms of hours and minutes. (This is why the box at the top of the duration column is labeled HH:MM.) If you prefer to measure the length of your exercise with a greater level of precision, you can choose from six other options. Each option offers a different combination of the following units: hours (HH), minutes (MM), seconds (SS), and hundredths of seconds (hh). To change duration properties, click on the box at the top of the duration column until the option you want to use appears.

EXERCISE

Suggestions for Use

Estimating Intensity

Life Form calculates the calories you burn from exercise using both intensity and duration. Intensity represents your level of exertion, or the amount of work and therefore energy you require from your body. The higher your intensity, the more calories you burn. We've assigned a default intensity for each predefined exercise, which represents an average intensity for adults. Because we are all different and exercise in different ways, the default intensities might not be accurate for you. You can check an intensity for accuracy by measuring your heart rate while exercising (*Exercise H.R.*) and then making the following calculation:

If you don't remember your resting and maximum heart rates, select Edit User from the File menu to view them in your User Setup.

$$Intensity = ((Exercise\ H.R. - Resting\ H.R.) / (Maximum\ H.R. - Resting\ H.R.)) \times 10$$

While this formula might seem confusing, it makes more sense if you understand the relationship between intensity and heart rate. In a nutshell, intensity represents a percentage of the difference between resting heart rate and maximum heart rate. Life Form assumes your intensity at your resting heart rate to be 0.0 and your intensity at your maximum heart rate to be 10.0. Therefore, an intensity of 4.0 represents 40% of the difference between the two values.

If the intensity you calculate for an exercise is different than the intensity we've assigned, you can change the default number to reflect your personal performance. To edit the intensity for an exercise, follow these steps:

1.   From the Exercise menu, choose Edit Exercise. The Edit Exercise dialog box appears.

2.   Select the exercise you want to edit from the list by clicking on it.

3.   Choose Edit.

4.   Enter a new intensity in the Default Intensity text box.

5.   Choose OK. Life Form now calculates calories burned based on the new intensity.

Tracking Exercise Progress

If you are trying to get in shape, increase your stamina, or improve your performance, you can use the Exercise Journal to track progress toward your goal. The simplest method for viewing changes in your exercise performance is to scroll up and down through the Exercise Journal and note changes in time, distance, and intensity over time. You can print your Journal to view a greater range of exercise data more easily. You can also graph your progress using the Graphs page. Before you create your graph, you might want to add a goal item on the Measurements page. This will provide a standard against which you can measure your actual performance. If, for example, you want to increase the distance you run from 5 to 10 miles over the course of six months, you can create a Running Goal item following the steps outlined in *Creating a Goal Item* in *Chapter 7, Ratings*.

Using Other Sources of Calorie Calculations

Some exercise machines display an estimate of the number of calories you burn while using them. If you want to use an equipment manufacturer's numbers rather than Life Form's, you can replace the calculated value in the Calories field. Before you do this, however, you should be aware how Life Form makes its calculations. The number of calories Life Form displays reflects *only* the number of calories burned from exercising. It does not include the calories you burn to stay alive during your exercise session, or in other words, BMR calories. This is because you receive credit for your basal metabolic rate elsewhere in Life Form. Because the numbers equipment manufacturers provide might include BMR calories, using these numbers could add extra calories to your Exercise Calories and Daily Metabolism Estimate.

Tracking General Activity as Exercise

If you spend a day removing a stump from your backyard or painting your house, you will probably burn more calories than you do on a regular day. Similarly, if you are a weekend gardener, you probably expend more energy on weekends than you do during the work week. If you haven't accounted for these types of activities in the Lifestyle Activity component of your Activity Level Setup, you will not get credit for the extra calories you burn in your Daily Metabolism Estimate. You can avoid this problem by tracking activities that you would not normally consider "exercises" in the Exercise Journal. Add any activities that you engage in regularly or even on a one time basis to the Exercise list to improve the accuracy of your Daily Metabolism Estimate. Examples of possible activities are yard work, moving furniture, and mopping floors.

Resetting Your Activity Level

You can compare the number of calories you burn to the number of calories you consume by viewing calorie calculations on the Exercise and Food pages or using the Calories graph. (For instructions on using the Calories graph, see the *Suggestions for Use* section of *Chapter 9, Graphs*.) If you discover that your calories burned exceed your calories consumed, but you are not losing weight, you might have overestimated your Activity Level. Similarly, if your calories consumed exceed your calories burned, but you are not gaining weight you might have underestimated your Activity Level. If you find such a discrepancy, you can compensate for the difference by adjusting your Activity Level.

To change your Activity Level, select Edit User from the File menu. Then click on the Activity Level Setup button. After the Activity Level Setup appears, select different options in the Activity, Women Only, Eating Habits, and Nervous Energy group boxes to increase or decrease your total Activity Level. Life Form will display the new estimate of lifestyle calories burned in the Daily Metabolism Estimate group box for the current date and all future dates.

Note: When you change your Activity Level, Life Form makes the change as of the date you enter it. It does not apply the change to past dates, so it will not affect previous calculations of calories burned.

EXERCISE

Notes

Entering Times and Dates in Life Form

Dates

Each time you enter an exercise, meal, or event in Life Form, you include a date with your entry. While entering a date might not seem like a difficult task, Life Form gives you a number of shortcuts to make it quicker and easier. Each date you enter must include a month, a day, and a year, and fall between January 1, 1880 and December 31, 2049. The month you enter is represented by a number 1-12, while the day is represented by a number 1-31. Life Form assumes the entry to be for a year in the twentieth century unless you specify otherwise. The month, day, and year fields are separated by forward slashes (/). You can move to the next field by typing a forward slash and back and forth between fields using the left and right arrow keys.

While the most common method for entering dates is to type a number in each field, you can type + to move the date forward by one day and - to move it back by one day. You can also type the following keys in any of the date fields to choose a date:

Key	First Time (Sets date as...)	Subsequent Times (Sets date as...)
M or m	First day of current month	First day of previous month
H or h	Last day of current month	Last day of next month
Y or y	First day of current year	First day of previous year
R or r	Last day of current year	Last day of next year
W or w	First day of current calendar week	First day of previous calendar week
K or k	Last day of current calendar week	Last day of next calendar week
T or t	Today	

If you prefer to view dates in calendar format, you can click on the button to the right of a date field to display the calendar. When you open the calendar, it displays the month containing the date currently in the date field. (Unless you've already edited it, this will be the current date.) You can use the buttons at the top of the calendar to change the year and month. You can select a day by clicking on it or using the arrow keys. Once you've chosen a date, click on the button to the right of the date field or anywhere outside the calendar to close it.

Times

In addition to entering a date, you will need to enter a time for your meals and certain items on the Measurements, Chemistry, and Ratings pages. Life Form measures time in hours and minutes or hours, minutes, and seconds. Valid times range from 12:00:00 am to 11:59:59 pm. The hour, minute, and second fields are separated by colons (:). You can move between these fields by pressing the colon key. When in a time field, you can type a number or use the following keys as shortcuts:

Key	Action
N or n	Sets time to current time.
A or a	Selects am option.
P or p	Selects pm option.

Calculating Energy Expenditure

Life Form can help you to better understand the relationship between your eating habits, your energy expenditure, and your weight. If you enter your meals using the Food page, the program automatically calculates the calories you consume on a daily, weekly, or monthly basis. By using the Activity Level feature and entering your exercise on the Exercise page, you can help Life Form to estimate the number of calories you burn at these same intervals. Once the program calculates these values, you can use the graph and report features to look for correlations between your weight and your net calorie expenditure.

Basal Metabolic Rate (BMR)

Life Form estimates your daily calorie expenditure by taking a number of factors into account. The first is your basal metabolic rate, or BMR. Your BMR represents the minimum amount of energy required to keep your body functioning while resting. This includes energy used for maintaining heartbeat, respiration, and body temperature. Life Form calculates your BMR using the Harris-Benedict equation, a method commonly accepted by exercise physiologists. The Harris-Benedict equation takes into account height, weight, and age in the following manner:

Men
BMR = 66.5 + 13.8(Weight(kg)) + 5(Height(cm)) - 6.76(age)

Women

BMR = 665 + 9.5(Weight(kg)) + 1.8(Height(cm)) - 4.7(age)

Children

BMR for children is calculated using the formula for men. When a child turns 13, Life Form uses the gender-appropriate formula.

Activity Level

If you were a car, your BMR would be the amount of energy you used when idling. Like automobiles, most of us rev up our engines at some point during the day and burn fuel to get from one place to another. The average very sedentary person burns an additional 30% of their BMR over the course of a normal day. This figure includes energy used to digest food, energy used to respond to cold, stress, and other external stimuli, and calories burned in conducting our normal daily activities. To compensate for differences in individual energy expenditure, Life Form provides the Activity Level questionnaire. The program uses the responses you provide in this questionnaire to calculate a caloric expenditure specialized to reflect the characteristics of your individual lifestyle.

When you create a new user or edit an existing user's setup, Life Form displays the User Setup dialog box. An Activity Level appears near the bottom of this box. The Activity Level represents the percentage of your BMR that you burn in addition to your BMR over the course of a normal day. If you do not go through the Activity Level Setup, Life Form leaves this number at 30, or in other words, gives you credit for burning an additional 30% of your BMR in your day-to-day activities. If you want to tailor the Activity Level to reflect your personal lifestyle, click on the Setup button. Life Form displays the Activity Level Setup dialog box that allows you to enter information specific to you.

Your Activity Level comprises four or five different components, depending on your gender. If you are a male, Life Form assigns values for your lifestyle, eating habits, nervous energy, and exercise, based upon the responses you provide in the questionnaire. If you are a female, you can also receive credit for pregnancy or lactation. Your *Weekly Lifestyle Activity Excluding Exercise* is your original 30 plus the sum of the four lifestyle components, namely, *Activity, Eating Habits, Nervous Energy,* and *Women Only. Exercise Activity* is a value derived from the number of hours you exercise each week. Your T*otal Activity Level*, then, is the sum of your *Weekly Lifestyle Activity Excluding Exercise* and *Weekly Exercise Activity.*

Weekly Lifestyle Activity Excluding Exercise

Activity

The first set of radio buttons in the Activity Level Setup dialog box allows you to compensate for the number of calories you burn on the job and around the house. If you spend most of the day sitting down, rarely get up to perform tasks, and avoid walking whenever possible, your activity qualifies as *very sedentary* and you do not receive any additional credit toward your Weekly Lifestyle Activity. If your daily activity can be described as anything other than very sedentary, Life Form adds points to your Weekly Lifestyle Activity.

You should choose *Sedentary* if you spend most of your day sitting at a desk or on a couch and don't get up much. Examples of sedentary professions are computer programmer and telephone operator. Life Form adds 10 points to your Lifestyle Activity if you select the Sedentary rating. You should choose *Lightly Active* if you spend a good part of your day standing. Examples of lightly active professions are floor salesman and nurse. You receive 20 points toward your Weekly Lifestyle Activity if you choose the Lightly Active rating. If you spend most of your day on your feet or engaged in moderate physical activity such as walking short distances, you should choose *Active*. Examples of active professions are mailman, maid, and waitress. Life Form adds 30 points to your Weekly Lifestyle Activity for an Active rating. If you spend most of your day engaged in heavy physical activity, such as walking long distances or lifting and carrying boxes, you should choose *Very Active*. Examples of very active professions are carpenter, meatpacker, and carpet layer. You receive 60 points toward your Weekly Lifestyle Activity for a Very Active rating. You should choose *Strenuously Active* if you spend most of your day engaged in very heavy physical activity, such as running or carrying heavy objects. Examples of strenuously active professions are lumberjack and bicycle courier. The strenuously active receive 100 additional points toward their Weekly Lifestyle Activity.

Women Only

Below the occupational level is a box for women to check if they are lactating or pregnant. The USDA suggests you eat 300 additional calories per day while pregnant and 500 while nursing. Life Form will add 25 points to your Weekly Lifestyle Activity for pregnancy and 35 points if you are nursing.

Eating Habits

Your body expends approximately 8-10% of the calories you consume in the digestion and absorption of the foods you eat. The more food you eat, the more energy your body uses. Life Form includes this expenditure, known as the thermic effect of food, in your basal metabolic rate. If you are an average eater, Life Form assumes the basic BMR calculation to be accurate. If, however, you eat significantly more or less than the average person of your size and gender, Life Form adjusts your Weekly Lifestyle Activity to account for the subsequent difference in energy expenditure. Life Form assumes *average* eating habits to be 2000 calories per day for women and 2500 calories per day for men. If you eat infrequently or only in very small amounts, you should choose *very light*. Very light eaters receive a 10 point deduction from their Weekly Lifestyle Activity. Those with *light* eating habits consume more than very light eaters, yet about 25% less than average eaters and receive a 5 point deduction. Consider your eating habits *heavy* if you eat more often or in greater amounts than the average person. Life Form adds 5 points to the heavy eater's Weekly Lifestyle Activity. Your eating habits are *very heavy* if you consume extra large portions and possibly four to five full meals per day. Life Form assumes very heavy eaters' caloric intake to be approximately 50% greater than average eaters' and assigns them a 10 point Weekly Lifestyle Activity increase.

Nervous Energy

The amount of energy you burn each day is also dependent upon your level of nervous energy. The more you fidget, the more calories you burn. If you continually exhibit nervous energy through behaviors such as pacing, tapping your toes, or rocking back and forth, you should select *Very Fidgety* from the list of options. Life Form assigns 20 additional points to your Weekly Lifestyle Activity for this selection. If you are frequently, but not always, restless or fidgety, *Fidgety* is the appropriate choice. Those falling into this category receive a 10 point addition to their Weekly Lifestyle Activity. *A Little Fidgety* refers to people who get a little antsy every now and then, but for the most part are relaxed. Life Form gives you five additional Weekly Lifestyle Activity points for this rating. If you describe yourself as generally relaxed, choose *Calm* from the list. Life Form makes no change to your Weekly Lifestyle Activity for this selection.

Weekly Exercise Activity

The final area of Activity Level is your exercise estimation. This is the one area where you have direct control over your caloric expenditure. It is doubtful anyone would want to become a heavy eater just to gain the advantage of digesting the extra food. And few of us strive to be stressed in an attempt to increase our energy expenditure. Our level of exercise, however, can and does change over the course of our lives. For most of us the motivation behind these changes comes from within. While Life Form has an Exercise page to record your actual exercises, this portion of the Activity Level questionnaire allows you to quickly estimate your weekly exercise.

Be sure to note that you should enter weekly rather than daily values in the Exercise Activity section. If, for example, you walk an hour a day and play racquetball once a week for an hour, you should enter 7 hours in light or medium exercise and 1 hour in heavy exercise. *Light* exercises include activities falling into the 0.1-3.9 range for intensity level, such as golf, bowling, and average walking. *Medium* exercises raise your heart rate to the lower end of the aerobic training zone, or the 4.0-6.9 range for intensity level, and include fast walking, badminton, and dancing. *Intense* exercises raise your heart rate to the upper end of the aerobic zone, or intensity levels between 7.0 and 9.9, and include running, aerobics, and cross country skiing. Life Form adds 1.5 points to your Exercise Activity for each hour of light exercise, 3 points for each hour of medium exercise, and 6 points for each hour of intense exercise. This number is a rough estimate and Life Form will use it to calculate your Daily Calorie Expenditure Estimate. When you enter your exercises on the Exercise page, Life Form gives you the option of calculating this number using actual values rather than the Exercise Activity estimate.

Actual Exercise Calories

Life Form uses a basic model for calculating energy expenditure from exercise. Each exercise has been assigned a default intensity level between 0.1 and 9.9 that is set to match the average caloric expenditure for that exercise. (See the *List of Exercises* later in this chapter for default values.) When you enter an exercise and a duration, Life Form automatically calculates your calories burned from the exercise. You can personalize these results, however, by altering the default intensity to reflect your personal habits. If, for example, you play tennis with your four-year-old, you may want to reduce the default intensity level to account for your decreased activity. If, on the other hand, you play with the club pro, you should probably increase the intensity level to account for the additional energy you will expend.

An added feature of Life Form allows you to track your exercise according to heart rate rather than intensity. Though the two are indicative of the same thing, namely the amount of work you require from your body to perform the exercise, your heart rate is thought by some to be a more precise measure of your exertion than intensity. If you would like to enter your heart rate for a specific exercise, click on *Int.* in the title bar which changes the heading to

H.R. Enter your heart rate in the appropriate column. The default intensities take into account the standard work and non-work times associated with each exercise. Weightlifting for example, might be a 10 for the brief time you are actually pushing weight, however most of the time you are resting. Therefore the default is set closer to 4 or 5. You can change weightlifting to a 10, but if you do, make sure you only record the few minutes you are exercising or your exercise calories will be too high.

At the bottom of the Exercise page there are two group boxes. *Exercise Calories* contains items exclusively concerning exercise. *Daily Metabolism Estimate* comprises the data collected on the Activity Level Setup as well the daily calories for the date on the left hand side. Wherever the word *actual* appears, the data is from the exercises you entered on the exercise page. *Estimated* refers to the data you entered in the Activity Level Setup. In the Daily Metabolism Estimate box, you can toggle between *Estimated* and *Actual*.

Calculations

In order to calculate both your average daily calories and calories from exercise, Life Form uses your age, weight, height, sex, and Activity Level in a series of mathematical formulas. Though Life Form cannot calculate your exact caloric expenditures, by using these formulas and data, it can come much closer than generic tables, which do not include sex, weight, height, or age.

General Calculations

Life Form uses five basic values in calculating your lifestyle and exercise caloric expenditures: Exercise Level, Fitness Level, Body Mass Index, Volume Oxygen Maximum, and Basal Metabolic Rate.

Exercise Level
Your Exercise Level is the number of points you receive for Weekly Exercise Activity in the Activity Level Setup divided by 10.

Fitness Level
Your Fitness Level is your Weekly Lifestyle Activity (see *Activity Level Setup*) plus your Exercise Level divided by 10. Fitness Levels fall within a range of 0 - 7.

Fitness Level = (Weekly Lifestyle Activity + Exercise Level)/10

Body Mass Index (BMI)

The second formula is your Body Mass Index, or your weight in kilograms divided by your height in meters squared. Your body mass index provides a simple way for Life Form to calculate your body composition. Life Form uses your BMI to better calculate your calories from exercise.

$$BMI = Weight(k)/Height^2(m)$$

Volume Oxygen Maximum (VO$_2$ Max)

The next step uses BMI to calculate your Volume Oxygen Maximum (VO$_2$ Max). Your VO$_2$ Max is the amount of oxygen you consume when exercising at your maximal rate. Once again the formula is different for men and women.

Female

$$VO_2 \text{ Maximum} = (\text{Fitness Level} \times 1.951) - (\text{Age} \times .381) - (\text{BMI} \times .754) + 56.63$$

Male

$$VO_2 \text{ Maximum} = (\text{Fitness Level} \times 1.951) - (\text{Age} \times .381) - (\text{BMI} \times .754) + 67.35$$

(From the University of Houston Non-Stress Estimate of VO$_2$ Max. Developed at the NASA Space Center.)

Basal Metabolic Rate (BMR)

The fourth and final general calculation computes your Basal Metabolic Rate. Life Form uses the Harris-Benedict equation, which is a sex-bifurcated regression. The calculations for both men and women are shown here.

Men

$$BMR = 66.5 + 13.8(Weight(kg)) + 5(Height(cm)) - 6.76(age)$$

Women

$$BMR = 665 + 9.5(Weight(kg)) + 1.8(Height(cm)) - 4.7(age)$$

Children

BMR for children is calculated using the formula for men. When a child turns 13, Life Form uses the gender-appropriate formula.

Daily Metabolism Estimate

The Daily Metabolism Estimate is the sum of your BMR plus an increase for activity and your exercise calories.

Daily Metabolism Estimate = BMR + (Activity Level $\times$ BMR $\times$ .01) + (Exercise Level $\times$ BMR $\times$ .01)

If you change the exercise component of the equation to *actual*, Life Form uses values from the exercises you have entered for the day rather than an approximation based on your Activity Level Setup.

Exercise Calories

Life Form calculates the calories burned during an exercise by using your heart rate or perceived intensity. Each of Life Form's 50 predefined exercises has been assigned a default intensity that corresponds with the average adult's caloric expenditure. If you decide to alter the intensity or enter a heart rate, Life Form remembers that value the next time you enter the same exercise.

If intensity is the entered value for an exercise, Life Form will change it into heart rate for internal calculations. The conversion is a linear conversion between your resting heart rate and maximum heart rate. The value 0 represents resting heart rate, while 10 represents maximum heart rate. 4 represents 40% of the difference between the two values. Once heart rate is ascertained, Life Form calculates the percentage of VO_2 Maximum using the Exercise Heart Rate and your Maximum Heart Rate. The formulas for men and women are shown below.

Male
$\%VO_2Maximum$ = (Exercise Heart Rate - 73)/(Maximum Heart Rate - 73)

Female
$\%VO_2Maximum$ = (Exercise Heart Rate - 63)/(Maximum Heart Rate - 63)

Life Form then takes this percentage, multiplies it by your VO_2, and divides the product by 3.5 to calculate your METS. METS are a standard measurement of energy.

METS = VO_2 Maximum $\times$ $\%VO_2Maximum$/3.5

Using METS and your weight, Life Form calculates calories expended.

Gross Calories Per Minute = METS $\times$ Weight(kg)/60
(Recommended by the American College of Sports Medicine)

The calories per minute are a gross number, and since Life Form calculates your BMR separately, it subtracts your BMR for the duration of the exercise to arrive at a net figure.

Calories from Exercise per Minute = Calories Per Minute - BMR Calories per Minute

The fact that Life Form uses net calories from exercise will create different numbers than familiar tables and exercise machines you may use. While you can choose to override Life Form's calorie calculations, you should remember Life Form already allows you a certain calorie count per minute for your BMR as well as your lifestyle addition.

While the above calculations apply to all exercises, Life Form calculates calories for running and walking using special distance-related calculations. If you do not enter a distance for either of these exercises, the standard calculations apply. When data is entered in the distance field, the following calculations are used.

Running Calories = 90 x miles x weight(kg)/60
(90 replaces 100 in the standard formula to compensate for BMR and Activity Level additions.)

Walking Calories = 60 x miles x weight(kg)/60
(60 replaces 75 in the standard formula to compensate for BMR and Activity Level additions.)

(Some of the formulas used in making calorie calculations have been taken or adapted from Robert M. Ross and Andrew S. Jackson, *Exercise Concepts, Calculations, and Computer Applications*, Benchmark Press, 1990.)

List of Exercises

Exercise	Intensity	Units
Aerobics	7.0	
Backpacking	6.2	
Ballet	5.5	
Baseball	2.5	
Basketball	7.0	
Bowling	2.0	
Boxing	9.9	
Cycling	7.0	
Dancing	7.0	
Football	6.7	
Golf w/o Cart	3.0	Strokes
Golf with Cart	2.2	Strokes
Handball	8.0	
Health Rider	6.0	
Hiking	5.7	

Exercise	Intensity	Units
Hockey	6.9	
Horseback Riding	2.2	
Ice Skating	4.5	
Jogging	7.0	
Jumping Rope	8.0	
Karate	6.9	
Mountain Biking	8.4	
Nordic Track	7.0	
Ping Pong	2.3	
Racquetball	8.0	
Rock Climbing	7.5	
Rollerskating	4.5	
Rollerblading	4.5	
Rowing	6.7	
Rowing Machine	6.5	
Running	7.0	
Skiing, Downhill	4.2	
Skiing, Cross Country	7.5	
Snowboarding	5.7	
Soccer	8.0	
Squash	8.0	
Stairstepping	7.5	
Stationary Bike	6.0	
Swimming	7.0	
Tennis, Doubles	4.0	Sets
Tennis, Singles	6.0	Sets
Treadmill-Run	6.0	Miles
Treadmill-Walk	3.0	Miles
Volleyball	4.5	
Walking	5.0	
Water Aerobics	5.5	
Water Polo	8.0	
Water-Skiing	4.5	
Weightlifting	5.0	
Wrestling	9.4	

MEASUREMENTS

As you begin to take control of your health, you may find that your body begins to change. You may lose or gain weight, increase muscle tissue, decrease fatty tissue, or lower your blood pressure. You may become more aware of physiological changes such as variations in body temperature or resting heart rate. Life Form's Measurements page provides an easy way to track data relating to your body's shape, size, and form. Using the items in the Measurements list, you can keep a record of changes in your height and weight and even monitor fluctuations in your shirt or dress size.

This chapter explains how to track data and work with items in the Measurements list.

Basic and Advanced Features

The Measurements page is similar in form and function to both the Chemistry page and the Ratings page. For a description of Basic and Advanced Features, see *Chapter 7, Ratings.*

This is what the Measurements page might look like after you open a few items from the list.

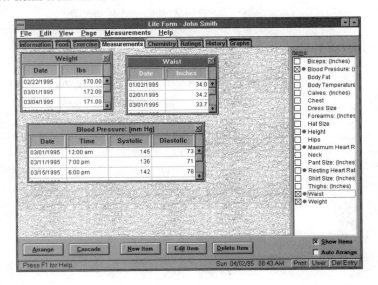

*Note: The **Height, Weight, Maximum Heart Rate,** and **Resting Heart Rate** items contain data as soon as you enter information in your User Setup. Because these items are linked to setup information, you cannot edit or delete them.*

Suggestions for Use

Tracking Changes in Your Weight

One of the items you can track on the Measurements page is your weight. Weight is a predefined item, and Life Form automatically tracks it based on the information you enter in the User Setup. The first entry in your Weight item is the weight you enter on the day you begin using Life Form. The program makes new entries in the item each time you edit your weight in the User Setup. If you prefer, you can record your weight loss or gain on the Measurements page, and Life Form will update your User Setup each time you enter a new weight.

Weight Goal is also a Measurements item. If you are trying to lose or gain weight, you can enter your goal weight in the Weight Goal item. (Enter it for the current date). You can then use the Weight graph on the Graphs page comparing Weight and Weight Goal to help you view your progress toward your goal. For more information on using graphs, see *Chapter 9, Graphs*.

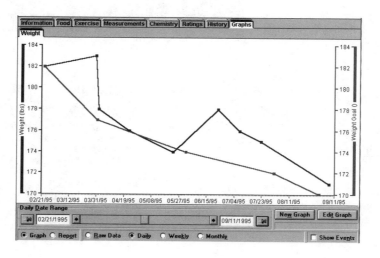

Creating a Goal Item

If you are trying to reach a goal for any of the items in the Measurements list, you can create a goal item to help you track your progress. To create a goal item on the Measurements page, see *Creating a Goal Item* in the *Suggestions for Use* section of *Chapter 7, Ratings*.

Tracking Changes in Body Composition and Size

If, like many of us, you are trying to get "in shape," one of your goals is probably to reduce your percentage of body fat and increase your percentage of muscle tissue. There are many different ways of measuring your progress in this regard. The most obvious is to measure your level of body fat. Various professionals can do this by performing a skin fold test with calipers or with more advanced techniques such as hydrostatic weighing. If your goal is not as much to lose body fat as to gain muscle, you can measure your neck, biceps, thighs, and waist to monitor increases in muscle size.

If you want to look for relationships between changes in your body size and composition and other factors in your life, such as diet and exercise, you can create graphs on the Graphs page. This graph includes *Biceps* and *Weightlifting:Duration*.

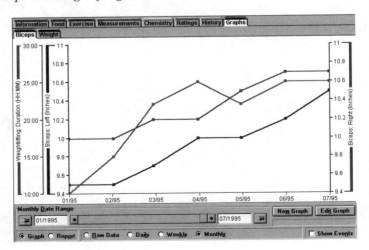

Keeping a Record of Clothing Sizes

Dress Size, *Hat Size*, *Pant Size* (waist and inseam), and *Shirt Size* (neck and sleeve) are all items in the Measurements list. If your sizes are changing because you're losing or gaining weight, or if your children's sizes are changing because they're growing, you might want to keep a record of these changes with the size items. Even if your sizes remain constant, you can record them to give to your spouse, or others shopping for you. If you do most of the family's clothes shopping, you can print the other member's items to make sure you have their current information.

Tracking Your Children's Growth

While you might not be getting any taller, your children probably are. The Measurements page gives you an easy way to track your children's growth, in terms of both height and weight. To begin tracking this information, you first need to set up each child as a user. When you do this, you will enter their starting weight and height in the User Setup. You can then enter changes periodically in the Height and Weight items on the Measurements page to create a record of their growth. If you want, you can create a graph on the Graphs page, like the one below, that shows their changes over time.

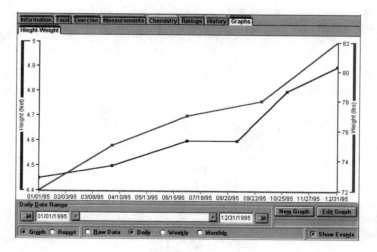

Tracking Blood Pressure

High blood pressure, or hypertension, is a medical problem that affects approximately 60 million Americans. If you are one of the 30 million who know of their condition (the other 30 million don't know), you probably have your blood pressure measured regularly. You can record your blood pressure on the Measurements page using the Blood Pressure item. The item contains two number fields, so you can enter both systolic (maximum) pressure and diastolic (resting) pressure. We've also included a time field so you can enter more than one measurement per day.

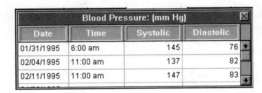

Blood Pressure: (mm Hg)				
Date	Time	Systolic	Diastolic
01/31/1995	6:00 am	145	76
02/04/1995	11:00 am	137	82
02/11/1995	11:00 am	147	83

You can look for causes and effects of high blood pressure by creating graphs on the Graphs page. A possible Blood Pressure graph could include items such as *Blood Pressure*, *Sodium*, and *Stress*.

Tracking Changes in Heart Rate

As you begin exercising more, a number of changes take place in your body. Your muscles get toned and your heart becomes stronger and more resilient. One effect of this conditioning might be that your resting heart rate decreases. If you want to track changes in your resting heart rate, you can make entries periodically in the Resting Heart Rate item on the Measurements page. Any changes you make to your resting heart rate on the Measurements page are also made to the Resting Heart Rate that appears in your User Setup.

Notes

Measurements Items

Item	Type	Units	First Subtitle	Second Subtitle
Biceps	DNN	Inches	Left	Right
Blood Pressure	DTNN	mm Hg	Systolic	Diastolic
Body Fat	DN	%		
Body Temperature	DTN	Degrees F		
Calves	DNN	Inches	Left	Right
Chest	DN	Inches		
Dress Size	DN	Size		
Forearms	DNN	Inches	Left	Right
Hat Size	DN	Inches		
Height	DN	Feet		
Hips	DN	Inches		
Maximum Heart Rate	DN	Beats/Min.		
Neck	DN	Inches		
Pant Size	DNN	Inches	Waist	Inseam
Resting Heart Rate	DN	Beats/Min		
Shirt Size	DNN	Inches	Neck	Sleeve
Thighs	DNN	Inches	Left	Right
Waist	DN	Inches		
Weight	DN	Pounds		
Weight Goal	DN	Pounds		

DN = Date, Number
DNN = Date, Number, Number
DTN = Date, Time, Number
DTNN = Date, Time, Number, Number

CHEMISTRY

In an effort to take control of their health, millions of Americans are paying close attention to the levels of certain chemicals in their bodies. Some track only blood cholesterol, while others carefully monitor iron, potassium, protein, and glucose levels in both their blood and urine. Periodic tests of blood and urine can prove a valuable tool in monitoring and treating conditions such as diabetes, anemia, and heart disease.

Life Form's Chemistry page provides an easy way to track the results of your blood and urine tests. By copying the figures from your lab report into the appropriate items, you can create an accurate record of your body's chemistry. You can use this record to gain a better understanding of how your body works and to keep your medical providers informed of changes in your health.

This chapter explains how to track data and work with items in the Chemistry list.

Basic and Advanced Features

The Chemistry page is similar in form and function to both the Chemistry page and the Ratings page. For a description of Basic and Advanced Features, see *Chapter 7, Ratings*.

This is what the Chemistry page might look like after you open a few of the items in the list.

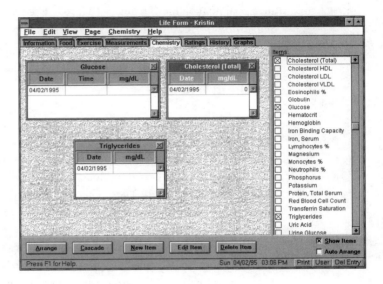

Suggestions for Use

Creating a Goal Item

If you are trying to reach a goal for any of the items in the Chemistry list, you can create a goal item to help you track your progress. To create a goal item on the Chemistry page, see *Creating a Goal Item* in the *Suggestions for Use* section of *Chapter 7, Ratings*.

Tracking Glucose

If you are diabetic, you probably measure your glucose daily with urine tests, blood tests, or both. Life Form gives you an easy way to keep a permanent record of your glucose levels. If you want to track your glucose, you can use the Glucose (blood glucose) and Urine Glucose items. These items are the Date, Time, Number type, so you can record your levels more than once a day.

You can also create a graph containing these items to help you look for trends or progress in controlling your glucose levels. If you are using diet or exercise to treat high glucose, you can include different items from the Food and Exercise pages in your graph to evaluate their effectiveness. Examples of items you might include are *Glucose*, *Total Carbohydrates*, and *Walking:Duration*.

Tracking Cholesterol

Most of us have had our blood tested to check our cholesterol level, and many of us even know our "number" or the number of milligrams of cholesterol per deciliter of blood. This number should be below 200, but for many Americans it creeps into the borderline (200-239) or abnormal (240 and above) range. Anything above 200 seems to indicate an increased risk for atherosclerosis, or hardening of the arteries, a condition which can lead to heart attacks, strokes, and other complications. If you have your cholesterol measured on a regular basis, you can use the Chemistry page to keep a record of your test results. Enter your "number" in the Cholesterol item after each test and soon you will have an accurate history of your blood cholesterol level.

If you are trying to control your cholesterol level through diet, exercise or medication, you can create a graph on the Graphs page to monitor your progress. A sample graph might include *Cholesterol* and *Saturated Fat* (from the Food page) and display the beginning of a prescription medication as an event from the History page.

Tracking Other Blood Fats

While many of us are familiar with cholesterol, we may not be aware that a normal blood cholesterol test measures not only our total cholesterol level (the number we usually know), but also the levels of high density lipoprotein (HDL) cholesterol and triglycerides. More detailed blood tests also measure the levels of low density lipoprotein (LDL) and very low density lipoprotein (VLDL) cholesterol. If you get a report from your lab or doctor including values for these different blood fats, you can enter them in the HDL, LDL, VLDL, and Triglycerides items. As with cholesterol, if your doctor prescribes medication or changes in diet or exercise to treat irregular levels of any of these blood fats, you can create a graph to monitor the effectiveness of the treatment. A sample graph might include *Triglycerides* and *Sugar* (from the Food page).

Tracking Ketones

If you are following a low-carbohydrate diet, you might want to monitor the level of ketones in your urine. The presence of ketones indicates your body is in a state of ketosis, and is expelling fat through urine and sweat. To monitor your ketones using Life Form, enter the results of your personal testing in the Urine Ketones item. You can enter one or many different values for each day. If you want to evaluate your ketone level in comparison to other factors, such as carbohydrates in your diet, you can create a graph on the Graphs page. A sample graph might include *Urine Ketones*, *Total Carbohydrates*, and *Sugar*.

Notes

Chemistry Items

Item	Type	Units
Albumin	DN	gm/dL
Basophils %	DN	%
Calcium	DN	mg/dL
Cholesterol Total	DN	mg/dL
Cholesterol HDL (High Density Lipoprotein)	DN	mg/dL
Cholesterol LDL (Low Density Lipoprotein)	DN	mg/dL
Cholesterol VLDL (Very Low Density Lipoprotein)	DN	mg/dL
Eosinophils %	DN	%
Globulin	DN	gm/dL
Glucose	DTN	mg/dL
Hematocrit	DN	vol %
Hemoglobin	DN	gm/dL
Iron Binding Capacity	DN	mcg/dL
Iron, Serum	DN	mcg/dL
Lymphocytes %	DN	%
Magnesium	DN	meq/dL
Monocytes %	DN	%
Neutrophils %	DN	%
Phosphorus	DN	mg/dL
Potassium	DN	meq/dL
Protein, Total Serum	DN	gm/dL
Red Blood Cell Count	DN	million/cmm
Transferrin Saturation	DN	%
Triglycerides	DN	mg/dL
Uric Acid	DN	mg/dL
Urine Glucose	DTN	mg/dL
Urine Ketones	DTN	mg/dL
Urine Protein	DTN	mg/dL
Urine Specific Gravity	DN	
White Blood Cell Count	DN	/cmm

DN = Date, Number
DTN = Date, Time, Number

RATINGS

The way you feel on any given day is likely the result of a wide variety of factors. Environmental conditions, physical symptoms, and psychological factors can all work together to determine whether you are happy or sad, tired or energetic. Life Form's Ratings page lets you track factors affecting your health and well-being so you can better understand the relationships between them. You can choose from the symptoms, habits, behaviors, and feelings included in the Ratings list or add your own.

This chapter explains how to track data and work with items in the Ratings list.

Basic Features

The first time you open the Ratings page, the screen looks a little empty. Life Form displays a list of items at the right and a few buttons along the bottom, but most of the screen remains blank. The empty area is reserved for displaying items you select from the list. There are over 60 items included in the list, which can grow as you add items of your own. A gray dot to the left of an item means that it already contains data. An "X" in an item's check box means it is open. The screen below shows that the Sleep and Stress items have been opened and that they contain data.

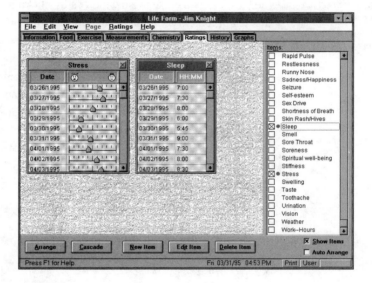

Deciding Which Items to Use

Before you begin entering data on the Ratings page, you need to decide which items you want to track. You can scroll through the list of items using the scroll bar to the right of the list. Select any item you are interested in monitoring by clicking on the check box to the left of the item name. When you do this, Life Form displays the item on the screen. You can select as many items as you like from the list, and should feel free to track anything you believe important in your life.

Showing and Hiding Items in the List

Life Form offers you many ways to change the appearance of the Ratings window. You can open and close item windows, arrange and cascade item windows, and hide, display, and resize the item list. By using these features, you can adjust the screen to best suit your personal needs.

✍An alternate method for arranging the windows is selecting Arrange from the Ratings menu.

If you know you want to track only certain items on the Ratings page, you can open the item windows you use and leave them open indefinitely. Click on the check box to the left of each item you want to monitor. Unless you close these windows by clicking on the check boxes in the list or the close buttons in the upper right corner of the item windows, Life Form will display these same items each time you return to the Ratings page. Once items are open on the screen, you can click on the Arrange button and Life Form will reposition the windows in an orderly fashion. If you want Life Form to automatically arrange the windows as you work, click on the Auto Arrange check box in the lower right corner of the screen. You can also cascade the windows by clicking on the Cascade button or choosing Cascade from the Ratings menu. The Ratings page below shows the Sleep, Irritability, Stress, Weather, and Indigestion items arranged on the screen.

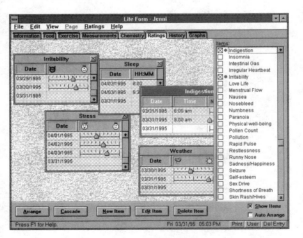

✍Click on the Show Items check box to close and open the Items list.

✍See Windows Skill 15 for more information on resizing windows.

You can hide the Items list and create more space to arrange your item windows by clicking on the Show Items check box located in the lower right corner of the Life Form window. You can change the size of the list by moving the left border to the left or right. To widen the list window, move the pointer over the left border of the list until the pointer is replaced by the resize symbol. Press the left mouse button and hold it down as you drag the mouse to the left. To narrow the list, follow the same procedure but drag the mouse to the right. This screen shows the same five items as the previous one, but the Items list is hidden.

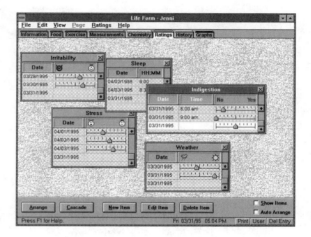

WINDOWS SKILL 15 — RESIZING WINDOWS

Sometimes you will want to keep a window on the screen, but change its size. To resize a window, move the pointer over the window frame so the resize arrow appears. Then hold down the left mouse button and move the edge of the frame to the desired location.

Entering a Record

All the Ratings items are similar in appearance, though there are variations in the number and titles of columns they contain. Each item displays titles at the top of the window and dates in the far left column. Records, or entries, in all items are listed by date, with the most recent

RATINGS

entry appearing at the bottom of the item window. The items stored on the Ratings page are similar in form and function to those of the Measurements and Chemistry pages. You can enter a record in an item by following these steps:

1. Open the item you want to use by clicking on its check box in the list. If the item is already open, click on the area below the last record entered. The focus moves to the date field of a new record.

The focus appears in the month area of the date field.

Weight	
Date	lbs
01/19/1995	124.00
02/01/1995	124.00
02/07/1995	126.00

✍Press + to move the date forward one day or - to move it back one day.

2. Enter the date in the date field, and then press Tab. Life Form displays the current date in the date field. If you are entering a record for the current date, you may tab to the next field.

✍See Windows Skill 16 for more information on sliders.

3. Enter the remaining information in the appropriate field(s). If the item is measured on a scale, use the slider to choose a value. Then press Enter. Life Form stores the entry and creates a new line in the item.

    Note: If you want to close the item after making the entry, click on the close box in the upper right corner of the item window or its check box in the Items list.

LIFE FORM TIP

Each item in the Ratings list has a predefined setup. The information you need to enter is described by the column headings that appear directly under the item name in the item window. For a list of the items and their setup information, see *Ratings Items* in the *Notes* section of this chapter.

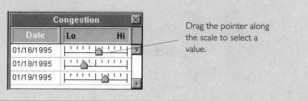
Inserting a Record

Life Form sorts records in an item according to date. If you are entering a record for the current date, you should follow the steps listed in *Entering a Record*. If you are entering a record that belongs between existing records, you can insert it in one of two ways. The first is to enter the record at the bottom of the item with the correct date, and Life Form will automatically move it to its proper spot. If you prefer to see the record in its correct place as you enter it, you can insert it by following these steps:

1.   Click on the record that will immediately follow the new record.

✍️*Or type Ctrl+I.*

2.   From the Edit menu, select Insert Entry. Life Form inserts a blank entry before the selected record.

3.   Enter information following the steps listed in *Entering a Record*.

        Note: If you insert a record out of date order, Life Form moves it to its proper spot in the item window.

Editing a Record

To edit any of the information entered on the Ratings page, click on the field you want to edit, type your changes, and press Enter. Life Form automatically stores the most recent changes without you having to press any additional keys.

Deleting a Record

✍Or type Ctrl+D.

To delete a record from an item, click on the record. Then click on the Del Entry button on the Status bar. (You can also click anywhere in the record and select Delete Entry from the Edit menu.)

Note: If you've selected an item but it doesn't appear on the screen because you've scrolled up or down in the item window, you cannot delete it. You can only delete a selected record if it is visible.

Adding a New Item

Life Form maintains a separate list of Ratings items for each user. You can add, edit, and delete items to and from this list according to your personal preferences. Any changes you make to your own Items list do not affect the lists of other Life Form users.

If an item you want to track is not included in the Ratings list, you can add it using the New Item button. To add an item to the Items list, follow these steps:

✍Or type Alt+N.

1. Click on the New Item button located near the bottom of the Life Form window. The New Item dialog box appears. (You can also select New Item from the Ratings menu.)

2.   Enter the title of the new item, and press Tab. You can enter a name of up to 30 characters, including spaces. The name may be more than one word.

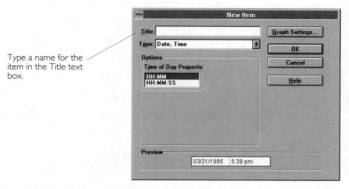

Type a name for the item in the Title text box.

3.   Select a type from the Type drop-down list box, and press Tab.

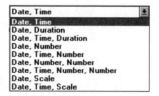

✍See the Notes section of this chapter for tips on choosing a type for an item.

There are nine types of items you can create. Each contains a field for the date and additional fields for some combination of the following variables: time, duration, number, and scale. Life Form displays a sample of the type you select in the Preview area of the New Item dialog box.

Most of the items you add on the Ratings page will be either the Date, Scale or the Date, Time, Scale type. Items requiring number field(s) will probably fall under Measurements or Chemistry, but can be added on the Ratings page if you like.

4.   Enter the requested information in the Options group box. Then press Tab.

When you choose *Date, Time*, you can choose from two different time-of-day options. HH:MM lets you record the time by the hour and minute, for example, 10:30. HH:MM:SS lets you add seconds to the times you enter.

RATINGS

When you select a type containing a *scale*, you can choose both the type of scale you want to use and the labels that will appear at either end of the scale. Select the scale type by clicking on one of the four options listed in the Scale group box. Each option is divided by hash marks into a different number of segments to help you measure your item. You can choose from a 1, 8, 10, or 20 scale. The 1 scale is useful when you enter the rating as a yes or no, as with nosebleeds. The other three options let you measure items with varying degrees of precision. If you do not choose from this list, Life Form displays the 10 scale.

✍For suggestions on choosing a scale type and labels, see the Notes section of this chapter.

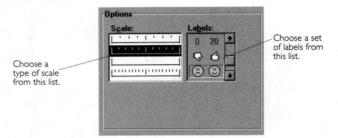

Choose a type of scale from this list.

Choose a set of labels from this list.

Choose the labels that will appear at the ends of the scale by clicking on one of the options in the Labels scroll box. If you do not choose from this list, Life Form displays the Lo/Hi labels.

When you select a type containing *duration*, Life Form lets you choose from seven different options. If you do not change the setting, Life Form automatically uses hours and minutes, or HH:MM. If you want to measure duration with a greater level of precision, you can choose one of the other six options, which offer different combinations of these units: hours (HH), minutes (MM), seconds (ss), and hundredths of seconds (hh). Select an option by clicking on it in the list.

When you select a type containing *at least one number field*, Life Form asks you to enter a unit of measure. If, for example, you wanted to add *Temperature* as an item, you could define the unit as *Degrees Fahrenheit*. The unit name appears as the column heading for the number field.

Note: You must assign a unit for items containing one or more number fields.

For items containing *one or two number fields*, you also need to specify a number of places to the right of the decimal. Life Form lets you record numbers up to five places to the right of the decimal point, or with accuracy ranging from whole numbers to ten thousandths. To assign the number of places, enter a number between 0 and 5 in the box labeled *Number of Places to the Right of Decimal*. If, for example, you added weight as an item and wanted to record changes in 1/4 pound increments, you would specify 2 as the number of places to the right of the decimal. Then you could record changes such as a drop from 125.50 to 125.25 to 125.00 pounds.

Weight	☒
Date	**lbs**
03/25/1995	125.50
03/28/1995	125.25
03/31/1995	125.00

If you select a type containing *two number* fields, enter a unit of measure and the number of decimal places as described above. This information will apply to both number fields. Assign titles to the two number columns in the First Subtitle and Second Subtitle text boxes. (The unit name you assign appears in parentheses after the item name in the item window.)

The unit you assign appears in the title bar of a Date, Number, Number item.

Calves: (Inches)		☒
Date	**Left**	**Right**
01/19/1995	12.0	12.7
02/19/1995	13.0	13.2
03/19/1995	13.2	13.5

The first and second subtitles appear as column heads.

Note: The names you assign to the subtitle fields must be different.

5. If you want to change the default graph settings, click on the Graph Settings button. The Initial Graph Settings dialog box appears.

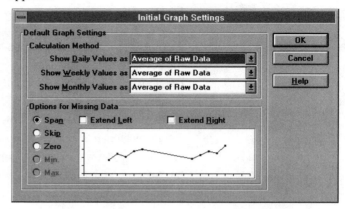

Edit the Calculation Method and Options for Missing Data to reflect your preferences. Then choose OK.

*Note: For a detailed explanation of all graph settings and options, see **Editing the Way an Item is Displayed in a Graph** in **Chapter 9, Graphs.***

6. Choose OK. Life Form adds the new item to the Items list.

Editing an Item

You may want to edit an item by changing its title, options, or graph settings. You can edit both the predefined items and those you add to the list by following these steps:

✍ *Or type Alt+I.*

1. Click on the Edit Item button located at the bottom of the screen. The Edit Item dialog box, which is identical in appearance to the New Item dialog box, appears.

2. Change the title, options, or graph settings by typing or selecting the corrected information.

3. Choose OK. Life Form stores the updated item.

Deleting an Item

If you want to shorten the list that appears on the Rating page, you can
delete the items you do not use from the list. To delete an item from the
list, follow these steps:

✍ *Or type Alt+D.*

1. Click on the Delete Item button located at the bottom of the
    program window. (You can also select Delete Item from the
    Ratings menu.) Life Form displays a warning like this one:

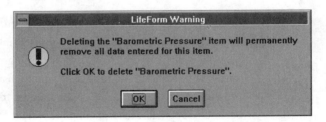

2. Choose OK. Life Form deletes the item from the Items list
    and deletes all data associated with the item.

    Note: If you decide later you want to add a deleted item back
    *to the list, follow the procedure described in **Adding a New***
    ***Item**. Refer to **Ratings Items** located in the **Notes** section of*
    this chapter for a list of default settings for the predefined
    items. If you add an item back to the list, you cannot retrieve
    any data you entered for the item before it was deleted.

Printing an Item

Life Form lets you print one item at a time from the Ratings page. All the records in an item are included. To print an item, follow these steps:

✍Or type Ctrl+P.

1.   Click on the window of the item you want to print. From the File menu, choose Print. The Print Dialog appears.

2.   Specify the date range you want to print by entering dates in the From and To text boxes. If you do not edit the beginning and ending dates, Life Form prints the entire item.

3.   Choose OK. Life Form prints your selection.

Advanced Features

Understanding Graph Settings

Each item you track on the Ratings page contains a group of settings that determine how data for the item is graphed or reported on the Graphs page. Life Form assigns the settings for the predefined items to provide good graphing results. If you are using only predefined items, chances are you won't give much thought to their graph settings. You can, however, edit these settings to reflect your personal needs and methods of recording data. If you want to change the graph settings for an item or are assigning settings for a new item, you can refer to *Deciding How Data Points are Calculated* and *Deciding How Missing Data is Graphed* in *Chapter 9, Graphs* for help.

Suggestions for Use

Creating a Goal Item

If, like most of us, you have set goals for yourself, you can use the Ratings page to track your success in reaching them. By creating a separate goal item for any of the items in the Ratings list or any item you add to the list, you establish a standard against which you can measure your actual progress. You can view your goal items and actual items side by side on the Ratings page or compare them on graphs you create using the Graphs page.

For a Constant Goal

Some goals are constant, or in other words, they do not change over time. You might, for example, decide that you want to get 8 hours of sleep each night. To create a goal item for a constant goal, follow these steps:

1. Click on the New Item button. The New Item dialog box appears.

2. Enter a title for your goal item, such as *Sleep Goal*.

3. From the Type drop-down list, select a type for the goal item. The type you select for the goal item should be the same as the corresponding item. If, for example, you are creating a Sleep Goal item, you should select *Date, Number* because *Sleep* is a Date, Number item.

4. Enter the requested information in the Options group box. The time-of-day properties, duration properties, units, places to the right of the decimal, type of scale, scale labels, and subtitles should match the settings for the actual item.

5. Click on the Graph Settings button. The Graph Settings dialog box appears.

6.   Click on the Extend Left and Extend Right radio buttons.

7.   Choose OK to close the Graph Settings dialog box.

8.   Choose OK. Life Form adds the goal item to the Items list.

Once you have set up the goal item, click on its check box to open the item. Enter the goal value or values as an entry for the current date. In the case of *Sleep Goal*, the item would look like this:

To view your progress, you can open the actual item and display it next to the goal item.

Though a constant goal item like this is not particularly useful when you are using the Ratings page, it can be very helpful in tracking your progress with a graph. When you create a graph including the actual item and the goal item, your goal appears as a straight line extending across the entire date range of your graph. If you have entered data in the actual item from day to day, the data approaches and moves away from this line, depending on your progress.

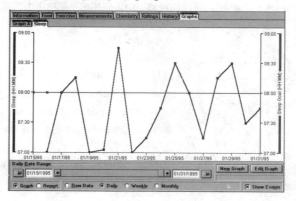

For a Gradual Goal

Many goals that you set for yourself represent a gradual change, such as losing 15 pounds by October 31. (*Note: **Weight Goal** is already an item on the Measurements page, but will be used here as an example of a gradual goal item.*) To create a gradual goal item such as a Weight Goal, follow these steps:

1. Click on the New Item button. The New Item dialog box appears.

2. Enter a title for your goal item, such as *Weight Goal*.

3. From the Type drop-down list, select a type for the goal item. The type you select for the goal item should be the same as the corresponding item. If, for example, you were creating a Weight Goal item, you should should select *Date, Number* because *Weight* is a Date, Number item.

4. If the Options group box appears after you select the type, enter the requested information. The units, places to the right of the decimal, type of scale, scale labels, and subtitles should match the settings for the actual item.

5. Click on the Graph Settings button. The Graph Settings dialog box appears.

6. In the Options for Missing Data group box, click on the Span radio button.

7. Choose OK to close the Graph Settings dialog box.

8. Choose OK. Life Form adds the goal item to the Items list.

    Once you have created the goal item, enter the actual value rather than a goal value for the starting date. Then enter milestones along the way to the final goal, or just the final goal and date you want to reach it.

The example below shows that you want to go from 165 pounds to 150 pounds over the course of six months.

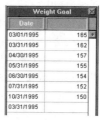

Weight Goal	
Date	
03/01/1995	165
03/31/1995	162
04/30/1995	157
05/31/1995	155
06/30/1995	154
07/31/1995	152
10/31/1995	150
03/31/1995	

When you create a graph including the goal item, Life Form spans the gaps between the data. The line the program draws between your original weight and your goal weight shows you what your progress should be over time. If, for example, you wanted to get an idea of how much weight you should have lost by May 15, you could use the reference line to view the value for that date.

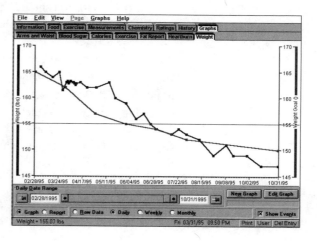

Tracking Specific Health Problems

Using the Ratings page, you can track a variety of symptoms associated with a specific health problem. If, for example, you are suffering from arthritis, you can track stiffness and soreness. If you suspect that the severity of your condition is related to the environment, you can track weather and barometric pressure. You may also experience emotional side effects of your illness that you want to monitor, such as irritability and frustration. If the arthritis interferes with your sleep, tracking sleep hours or quality can provide a valuable insight into the effects of the condition on your mind and body. Once you begin recording data for the items related to the health problem, you can use the Graphs page to more closely examine the relationships between them. You may also be able, with the assistance of your doctor, to find ways to alleviate or address specific symptoms.

For Women Only

Life Form's Ratings page provides an easy way to track different factors related to your menstrual cycle. Menstrual flow, cramping, fluid retention, and irritability are all predefined items in the Ratings list. You can add items for any other symptoms associated with your personal cycle, such as bloating. For each item important to you, record an intensity once a day every day during your menstrual or premenstrual cycle. This will create a complete history for each cycle. You can use this history to track patterns and abnormalities from month to month and to consult with your physician. For example, after reviewing your irritability and menstrual flow journals, you may conclude that the three days before the start of your flow are the worst of the month for irritability. If your cycles are regular, you can predict when these days will fall, and plan trips and special events around them.

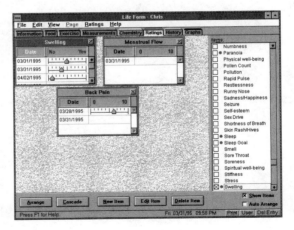

Tracking Biorhythm-Type Information

You may feel that certain aspects of your life are cyclical or rhythmic in nature. Perhaps you are always happy at the beginning of the month and sad at the end. Maybe you enjoy your work more on Thursdays than Mondays. Though you may not believe that how you feel on a given day hinges on your date of birth, you may notice consistencies in both your emotional and physical well-being. By tracking various items using the Ratings page, you can determine patterns in your behavior. This can help you to predict how you will feel during specific times and perhaps make plans accordingly.

Tracking Pollution

As members of an industrialized society, we are forced to inhale and ingest a wide variety of pollutants. While most of our bodies seem to tolerate this abuse, some are extra-sensitive to even the most common of toxins. If you suspect that smog, sulfur, carbon monoxide, or any other pollutants are making you feel badly, you can track them using the Ratings page. Nightly news programs often broadcast pollutant levels or ratings to help you along the way.

Notes

Defining an Item for Best Results

When adding an item to the Ratings list, you might be confused by the different types you can choose from. While the nine options can seem complicated, they are really quite simple. For each item you add, there is probably one type that works better than the rest. Before you decide which type you should assign an item, you can refer to the following explanations and examples:

Date, Time. Very few of Life Form's predefined items are Date, Time items. This is because you will usually want to attach more information such as numeric values or length of time to your entries. If, however, you want to keep track of certain symptoms or behaviors simply by noting the date and time of their occurrence, you can define them as Date, Time items. Fainting is an example of such an item. You probably wouldn't measure the length of a fainting incident or measure its severity on a scale. Instead, you would record the date and time it happened. You can also use *Date, Time* to keep track of items that occur regularly, but at different times from day to day, such as Daydreaming.

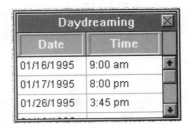

Date, Duration. When you want to track the number of minutes or hours that you engage in a particular activity, such as sleep or work, you can choose *Date, Duration*. Because this type does not include time, you wouldn't want to use it for activities you engage in more than once a day.

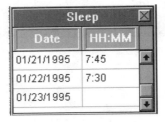

Date, Time, Duration. This type is helpful for tracking activities that you engage in more than once per day, such as daydreaming or reading. With *Date, Time, Duration*, you can create a history of these activities and the length of time you spend doing them.

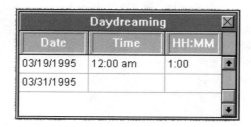

Date, Number. Most of Life Form's Date, Number items are found on the Measurements and Chemistry pages. For example, Body Fat, Height, and Weight are all Date, Number items. The number associated with this item type is usually an actual measurement taken with a yardstick, a scale, or, in the case of chemistry items, a laboratory machine.

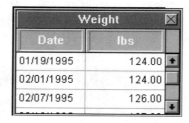

Date, Time, Number. Some items, such as blood glucose, are measured more than once per day. The Date, Time, Number type is useful for tracking such items, which can change from hour to hour or minute to minute.

Glucose		
Date	**Time**	**mg/dL**
01/06/1995	11:55 am	107
01/06/1995	6:00 pm	143
01/06/1995	10:00 pm	115

Date, Number, Number. This type is especially useful for the items you measure that come in pairs, such as biceps, forearms, thighs, and calves. Life Form includes the unit, such as inches, in the title of the item

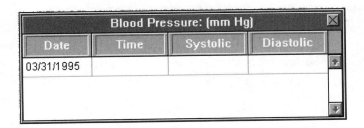

Calves: (Inches)		
Date	**Left**	**Right**
01/19/1995	12.0	12.7
02/19/1995	13.0	13.2
03/19/1995	13.2	13.5

Date, Time, Number, Number. Though relatively uncommon, the Date, Time, Number, Number type can be very useful. It works well for items that you measure in two different ways, such as blood pressure. As this example shows, you measure blood pressure in terms of both systolic and diastolic pressure.

Blood Pressure: (mm Hg)			
Date	**Time**	**Systolic**	**Diastolic**
03/31/1995			

Date, Scale. Most of the predefined Ratings items include a scale. Scales work well for items that you judge rather than measure. The Date, Scale type helps you rate items that affect you throughout the course of the day, rather than at specific times during the day. Stress and Sadness/Happiness are examples of Date, Scale items.

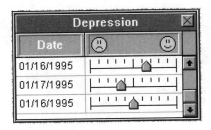

Depression	
Date	
01/16/1995	
01/17/1995	
01/16/1995	

Date, Time, Scale. This type is helpful for tracking items that you encounter and rate more than once per day, such as appetite.

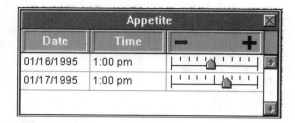

For those items you define as *Date, Scale* or *Date, Time, Scale*, you can choose both the number of segments the scale will contain and the labels that will appear at either end. You can specify that a scale contain 1, 8, 10, or 20 segments, depending on how precisely you want to measure your ratings. The more precise you want to be, the greater the number of segments you should choose. You will probably assess most items on a 10 scale. This is a scale that we are accustomed to using for rating everything from potential mates to the severity of headaches. If, however, you want to monitor an item more closely, you can choose a 20 scale. If you think of an item in more general terms, such as being "OK", pretty good", or "pretty bad", you might want to use an 8 scale. 1 scales are useful for items you want to track on a yes/no basis, or in other words, whether they occurred or not. For each scale you choose, you can slide the pointer along the scale to select a value located either on or between the tick marks.

Life Form gives you 14 different sets of labels to choose from when defining a scale. Though many of the labels reflect the same thing, you might have a preference for one set over another. If you're uncertain about which set to choose, you can use the following suggestions as a guideline.

Lo/Hi. These labels work well for items that you want to measure according to intensity or severity. If, for example, you are congested, you can enter the severity of your congestion by choosing a value somewhere on the scale between Lo and Hi.

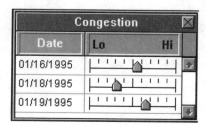

No/Yes. These labels work well with 1 scales for items you want to track by occurrence, such as nosebleeds. Each time you have a nosebleed, you can slide the scale all the way to the Yes end. If you want to track the days you don't have nosebleeds as well as those you do, you can make entries by sliding the scale to the No end.

Sliding the scale to the No end of the scale indicates you did not have a nose-bleed on a given day.

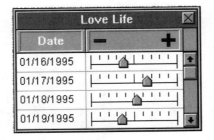

Sliding the scale to the Yes end indicates you had a nosebleed on a given day.

-/+. These labels are useful for items that range from bad to good, such as Love Life. An entry near the - end of the scale could indicate a break up or a fight, while an entry near the + end could reflect a romantic dinner or engagement. Most entries will probably fall some-where in the middle, however, with the center mark representing your status quo.

0/1. These labels work well with 1 scales and useful for items you want to measure on a gen-eral basis.

-1/1. These labels work well with 1 scales and serve a similar purpose as the +/- labels.

-5/5. These labels work well with 10 scales and offer an alternative to the +/- labels.

0/10. These labels work well with 10 scales. They provide an alternative to the Lo/Hi labels and are useful for items you tend to evaluate in numeric terms, such as pain. If, for example, you are trying to assign a value for your chest pain, you might have trouble deciding just where between Lo and Hi it falls. You might, however, be able to associate a number with your pain. Often doctors ask us to characterize our pain in these terms with questions like, "How bad is it on a scale of 1 to 10?"

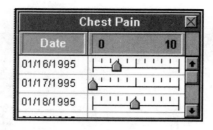

-10/10. These labels work well with 20 scale and serve the same basic purpose as the +/- labels

0/20. These labels work well with 20 scales and offer an alternative to the Lo/Hi and 1/10 labels.

Icons. The various sets of icon labels represent ranges of different qualities like bad to good, sad to happy, stressed to calm, and stormy to sunny. You can use the icon labels any time you feel they apply or are descriptive of an item.

These icons indicate a range of values from sad to happy.

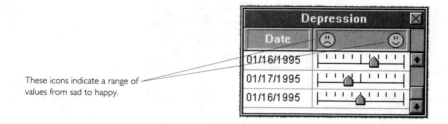

You might want to change the label we've assigned to an item, depending on what it is you want to measure. For example, we've defined *Insomnia* as a 1 scale with Yes/No labels. We've done this so you can record whether you had insomnia on a given day or you didn't. If you'd prefer to measure the severity of your insomnia from day to day, you might want to change the labels to Lo/Hi or 0/10.

Ratings Items

Item	Type	Units	Scale Type	Labels
Anger	DS		10	Lo/Hi
Anxiety	DS		10	Icons
Appetite	DTS		10	-/+
Back Pain	DS		10	0/10
Barometric Pressure	DN	Inch Hg		
Bedtime*	DS		10	-/+
Chest Pain	DS		10	0/10
Confusion	DS		10	Lo/Hi
Congestion	DS		10	Lo/Hi
Constipation	DS		10	Lo/Hi
Cough	DS		10	Lo/Hi
Cramping	DS		10	No/Yes
Depression	DS		10	Icons
Diarrhea	DS		10	No/Yes
Dizziness	DTS		10	No/Yes
Earache	DS		10	0/10
Emotional Well-Being	DS		10	Icons
Eye Irritation	DS		10	Lo/Hi
Fatigue	DTS		10	Lo/Hi
Fluid Retention	DS		10	Lo/Hi
Frustration	DS		10	Lo/Hi
Headache	DTS		10	No/Yes
Heartburn	DS		10	0/10
Hot Flashes	DTS		10	0/10
Indecisiveness	DS		10	No/Yes
Indigestion	DTS		10	No/Yes
Insomnia	DS		10	No/Yes
Intestinal Gas	DS		10	0/10
Irregular Heartbeat	DTS		10	No/Yes
Irritability	DS		10	Icons
Love Life	DS		10	-/+
Menstrual Flow	DS		10	0/10
Nausea	DS		10	Lo/Hi
Nosebleed	DTS		10	No/Yes
Numbness	DS		10	No/Yes
Paranoia	DS		10	No/Yes
Physical Well-Being	DS		10	0/10
Pollen Count	DS		10	Lo/Hi

Item	Type	Units	Scale Type	Labels
Pollution	DS		10	Lo/Hi
Rapid Pulse	DS		10	No/Yes
Restlessness	DS		10	-/+
Runny Nose	DS		10	No/Yes
Sadness/Happiness	DS		10	Icons
Seizure	DTS		10	No/Yes
Self-Esteem	DS		10	-/+
Sex Drive	DS		10	-/+
Shortness of Breath	DS		10	Lo/Hi
Skin Rash/Hives	DS		10	0/10
Sleep Hours	DD	HH:MM		
Smell	DS		10	Icons
Sore Throat	DTS		10	Lo/Hi
Soreness	DS		10	0/10
Spiritual Well-Being	DS		10	-/+
Stiffness	DS		10	0/10
Stress	DS		10	Icons
Swelling	DS		10	No/Yes
Taste	DTS		10	Icons
Temperature	DN	Degrees F		
Toothache	DS		10	0/10
Urination	DS		10	Icons
Vision	DTS		10	Icons
Weather	DS		10	Icons
Work Hours	DD	HH:MM		

DD = Date, Duration
DN = Date, Number
DS = Date, Scale
DTS = Date, Time, Scale

*You might be surprised that we've defined *Bedtime* as a Date, Scale item. You would probably expect it to be a Date, Time item, for which you enter the time you go to bed each night. While this seems to make sense, it creates problems if you want to graph bedtime. If you go to bed after midnight, what you consider your bedtime today is graphed on tomorrow's date. To avoid this problem, we've assigned a 10 scale with -/+ labels. If you assume the middle value to be 12:00 am, or midnight, then the tick mark to the left represents 11:00 pm and the tick mark to the right represents 1:00 am. This gives you a range of times from 8:00 pm to 4:00 am. If you always go to bed before midnight, you might want to delete *Bedtime* and recreate it as a Date, Time item.

HISTORY

The History page lets you record a wide variety of information having to do with your family's medical history. Presented in the form of a journal, it gives you a simple way to track doctor and dentist appointments, hospitalizations, illnesses, vaccinations, screening tests, medications, injuries, therapy, and any other information you believe important to your medical history. You can use the history you create to consult with your medical providers, seek second opinions, and track the course of your family members' individual medical conditions and treatments.

This chapter explains how to maintain a medical history using the History page.

Basic Features

The History page is a journal for recording events affecting your health. When you open the page, you will notice the screen looks like a page from a notebook. As you make entries over time, Life Form stores them by date. You can choose from 10 types of events, including *Doctor Visit, Dentist Visit, Hospital Visit, Therapy, Test, Medication, Vaccination, Illness,* and *Injury.* When you select a type of event, Life Form prompts you to enter information specific to that event. If you want to enter an event not included in the list, you can choose *Other Event* as the type and enter any information you feel important.

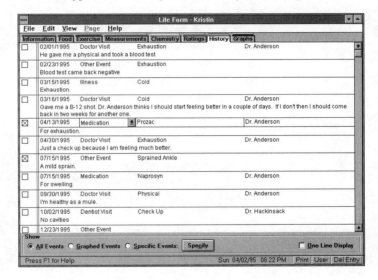

Entering an Event

After you open the History page, Life Form displays a blank entry at the bottom of the History and the focus appears in the date field of this entry. You can begin entering events by following these steps:

1.   Click on the date field of the blank entry if the focus is not already located there.

2.   Enter the date of the event, and press Tab.

3.   Select the type of event from the Event drop-down list box, and press Tab.

4.   Enter the requested information in the next one or two fields, depending on the type of event you select.

Each type of event requires different information. When you select *Doctor Visit, Dentist Visit*, or *Hospital Visit* or *Therapy* from the type list, enter the reason for your visit and the provider's name. If you select *Test, Medication*, or *Vaccination*, enter the name of the procedure or drug and the name of the referring doctor. *Illness, Injury*, and *Other Event* entries require only a name or description.

5.   If you want to include any additional comments, enter them as notes in the Notes field. You can use the Notes field to record any important information or details about the event, such as special circumstances or results.

6.   Press Enter. Life Form saves the event into the History.

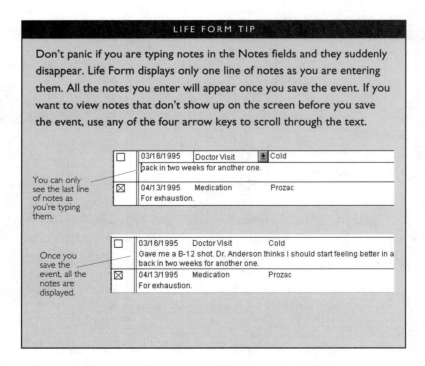

LIFE FORM TIP

Don't panic if you are typing notes in the Notes fields and they suddenly disappear. Life Form displays only one line of notes as you are entering them. All the notes you enter will appear once you save the event. If you want to view notes that don't show up on the screen before you save the event, use any of the four arrow keys to scroll through the text.

You can only see the last line of notes as you're typing them.

Once you save the event, all the notes are displayed.

Inserting an Event

Life Form stores records in the History according to date. If you are entering a record for the current date, you should follow the steps listed in *Entering an Event*. If you are entering a record that belongs between existing records, you can insert it in the History in one of two ways. The first is to enter the record at the bottom of the History, and let Life Form move it to its proper spot once you press Enter. If you prefer to see the record in its correct place as you enter it, you can insert it by following these steps:

1. Click on the record in the History that will immediately follow the new record.

✎ Or type Ctrl+I.

2. From the Edit menu, select Insert Entry. Life Form inserts a blank entry before the selected record.

3. Enter information following the steps listed in *Entering an Event*.

Note: If you insert a record out of date order, Life Form moves it to its proper spot in the History.

Editing an Event

To edit any of the information entered on the History page, click on the field you want to edit, type your changes, and press Enter. Life Form automatically stores the most recent changes without you having to press any additional keys.

Deleting an Event

To delete an event from the History, follow these steps:

✍️Or type Ctrl +D.

1.   Click on the record and press the Del Entry button on the Status Bar. (You can also click anywhere in the record and select Delete Entry from the Edit menu.) The following message appears:

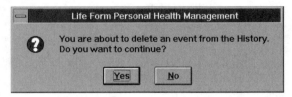

2.   Choose Yes. Life Form deletes the event from the History.

Marking Events to Be Graphed

You can include events from the History in the graphs and reports you create on the Graphs page. This can help you see the effects of major events such as pregnancy, injuries, and illnesses. The graph below shows two events displayed as vertical lines.

Events are displayed as vertical lines on a graph.

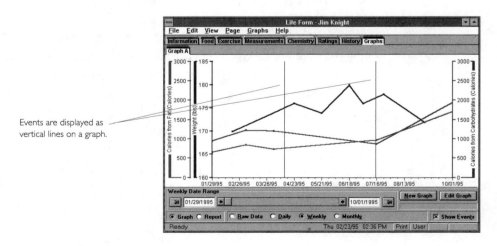

To include an event in your graphs and reports, click on the check box to the left of the date. You can exclude the event by deselecting the option (clicking on the check box again, so the "X" disappears).

If the check box for an event is selected, Life Form includes the event in your graphs.

☒	04/13/1995 Medication For exhaustion.	Prozac		Dr. Anderson
☐	04/30/1995 Doctor Visit Just a check up because I am feeling much better.	Exhaustion		Dr. Anderson
☒	07/15/1995 Other Event A mild sprain.	Sprained Ankle		
☐	07/15/1995 Medication For swelling.	Naprosyn		Dr. Anderson

If the check box for an event is not selected, the event will not appear in your graphs.

Viewing Only Graphed Events

Life Form lets you limit the events displayed on the History page to those you have selected for graphing. To choose this option, click on the Graphed Events radio button in the Show group box at the bottom of the Life Form window. This option is helpful if you want to view a particular group of items.

Using the One-Line Display

You can maximize the number of events Life Form displays by clicking on the One-Line Display check box also located in the Show group box. When you select one-line display, Life Form hides the Notes field of each entry. The Notes field still appears when you add a new event to the History, but it disappears as soon as you save the event.

To choose one-line display, click on the check box in the lower right corner of the program window. You can turn off the one-line display by clicking on the check box again so the "X" disappears.

When you choose the one-line display option, each event appears as a single line in the History.

HISTORY

Printing the History

To print your History, follow these steps:

✐Or type Ctrl+P.

1. Click on the Print button on the Status bar. (You can also select Print from from the File menu.) The Print dialog box appears.

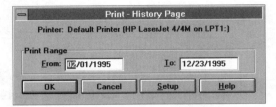

2. Specify the range of dates you want to print. If you do not change the beginning and ending dates, Life Form prints the entire History.

3. Choose OK. Life Form prints your selection.

Advanced Features

Viewing Specific Events

As you record events on the History page from month to month, your personal History will grow. At times you may want to view or print specific events that are connected in one way or another. For example, you might want to look at all your dental entries or only those entries related to a particular injury. Life Form allows you to control the events displayed in the History in two ways. First, you can select any type or combination of types from the list of 10 event types. If you want to view only your dentist visits, you can instruct Life Form to show only the Dentist Visit type entries. Second, you can specify words and phrases contained in the entries you want to view. If you want to view only those entries related to your ankle injury, for example, you can tell Life Form to display those events containing the word *ankle*.

To display specific events, follow these steps:

1.   If it is not shaded, click on the Specific Events radio button in the Show group window.

2.   Click on the Specify button. The Specify Events Shown dialog box appears.

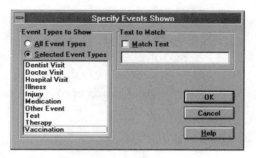

3.   Choose the type or types of events you want Life Form to display. If you want to include all types of events in your display, click on the All Event Types radio button. If you are specifying events from selected categories, click on the Selected Event Types radio button. Choose the type or types of events you wish to include by clicking on them in the list box.

✍Clicking an item in the list that is already highlighted deselects it.

4.   Specify any text you want the displayed events to contain. If you want to limit the events that appear in the History to those containing a common word or phrase, such as *headache*, click on the Match Text check box. Enter the text exactly as you have used it in your event entries in the text box provided.

5.   Choose OK. Life Form returns to the History, but displays only those events meeting the specifications you have just entered.

LIFE FORM TIP

You can restore the full History at any time by clicking on the All Events radio button. If, after returning to the full display, you reselect the Specific Events option, Life Form recalls the last set of specifications you entered and displays events accordingly.

Suggestions for Use

Using the History to Consult Doctors

If you have a specific health problem, your History can be a valuable resource in consulting doctors. If you use the History page to keep a record of all tests, medications, and medical visits by date, you can take a copy of this record to your doctors. In this way you can provide them with an accurate account of your illness or condition and any treatments you've tried.

Keeping a Record of Medications

If you've ever taken anything stronger than an aspirin to ease your pain or cure your cough, you know how confusing medications can be. Names, dosages, and special instructions such as "Take with food" and "Do not operate heavy machinery" are often complicated and sometimes the drugs they accompany don't even work for you. You can use the History page as a record of the medications you take over time. Not only can you record basic information, you can also note their effectiveness in treating your condition and any adverse reactions you may have to them. This information can be helpful for your doctor when deciding what to prescribe for you in the future. If you are being treated over the long term, this can also help you monitor progress and changes in your treatment.

If you want to view a history of your medications, you can limit the display of events to the Medication type. You can print this record for personal reference or to show your medical providers.

Keeping a Record of Screening Tests

Your doctor or other health professional is likely to recommend that you undergo various screening tests on a regular basis. These tests include blood cholesterol screens, thyroid function tests, and mammograms and help to detect heart disease, cancer, and other illnesses. You can use the History page to keep track of these tests and any others your doctors recommend by entering them as events in the Test category. By entering the date, type, referring doctor, and results of each test, you can create an accurate record of screening tests. This can help you to monitor changes in specific conditions and will be useful if you change doctors or apply for life or health insurance.

You can view a history of your screening tests by limiting the events displayed to *Test* events. If you want to give a copy of your screening test information to your doctor or insurance company, print the History.

Keeping a Record of Your Children's Vaccinations

Children in the United States are required to complete a series of vaccinations before entering school. If you have set up your children as Life Form users, you can use the History page to keep a record of their vaccinations. Whenever one of your children is vaccinated, record the vaccination as an event in the child's History. Choose Vaccination as the type of event and enter the type of vaccine, for example, measles or rubella, as well as the name of the doctor or agency administering it. You can record any reactions the child has to the vaccine in the Notes field. Although your child's Life Form History is not official proof of vaccination, it can provide a valuable reference when filling out medical, school, or insurance forms. For convenience, you can print a copy of each child's vaccination history.

Notes

Logic for Specifying Events

The Specify option provides you with two methods for defining the events Life Form displays in the History. You can limit events shown both by type and by text, as explained previously in this chapter. If you choose both options, Life Form restricts the events displayed to those meeting both criteria. For example, if you select *Medication* from the Selected Event Types list box and enter *Penicillin* in the Match Text box, Life Form shows only the Medication events containing the word *Penicillin*.

GRAPHS

The information you record on Life Form's various pages can reveal important facts about you and your health. The Graphs page makes it easy to create graphs and reports that include data from different pages, so you can look for trends and view your progress.

This chapter explains how to create and edit graphs and reports.

Basic Features

At first glance, Life Form's Graphs page can seem complicated, but you shouldn't be intimidated by its appearance. The program automatically creates three graphs for you, and you can create and use additional graphs by following a few simple steps.

When you open the Graphs page, you will see three tabs at the top of the page, each representing a graph. The Calories graph compares the number of calories you burn and the number of calories you consume; the Vitamins graph plots data for the amounts of Vitamin A, Vitamin C, Calcium, and Iron in your diet; and the Weight graph compares your actual weight with your weight goal. For more information on these graphs, see the *Suggestions for Use* section of this chapter. The Calories graph below will help you understand the different areas of the Graphs page and the basic elements of a graph.

Life Form displays a tab for each graph you create. You can open a graph by clicking on its tab.

This graph shows data for one week. If you create or open a graph before you've entered much data, it might look empty compared to this one.

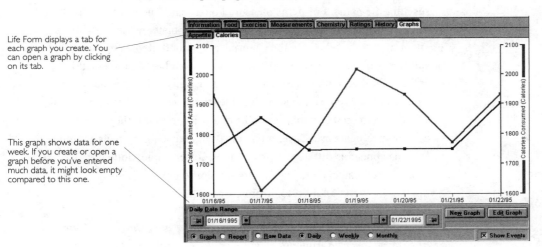

These are the things you see on the screen after opening a graph:

Tabs. When you open the Graphs page, Life Form displays another set of tabs below the main page tabs. Each tab belongs to a graph and shows the name of the graph. You assign the name of the graph when you create it. The title *Calories* appears on the tab for the example Calories graph. You move from graph to graph using these tabs just as you move from page to page in the program.

Items List. On the right side of the program window, Life Form displays a list of the items you can include on your graphs. These items come from the Food, Exercise, Measurements, Chemistry, and Ratings pages, as well as the Activity Level Setup. You can select up to six items from the list. In the example, *Calories Burned(Actual)* and *Calories Consumed* are selected.

Dates. Life Form displays dates along the bottom of the graph. The program automatically assigns beginning and ending dates for a graph, but you can change these dates if you like. The example shows data for 7 days.

✎Item labels can include a name, unit, scale, and legend.

Labels. Labels for the items you include in the graph appear along one or both sides of the graph, depending on how many items you select. You can include up to six items in each graph. Each label contains the *name* of the item, the *unit* by which the item is measured, a scale, and a legend. If units have been assigned to an item, they appear in parentheses after the name. For items measured on a scale, such as *Stress* or *Love Life*, Life Form displays the symbols associated with the scale at either end of the label. On the Calories graph, both items appear in calories. Life Form assigns a *scale* for each item based on the data entered for that item. In this Calories graph, daily calorie values range from 1600 to 2100, so the scale includes these values. The *legend* identifies an item on the graph. If you have a color monitor, the legend for each item appears as a different color. If you have a gray scale monitor, legends appear as different types of lines, for example, dotted or dashed. You can change legends from color to gray scale by deselecting the Show in Color option from the Graphs menu.

Note: When you print a graph on a non-color printer, the legends and lines are converted from different line colors to different line types. Color printers print graph lines as they appear on a color monitor.

LIFE FORM TIP

If you have a gray scale monitor, you need to deselect the Show in Color option. You can do this by clicking on Show in Color in the Graphs menu. If you do not turn off this option, all the lines on your graphs will look the same.

Controls. Below the graph are a series of controls that help you further define your graph. Life Form displays four radio buttons that allow you to choose from Raw Data, Daily, Weekly, or Monthly values. The Calories graph example shows Daily values. There is a control for setting the time range of the graph, buttons for making a new graph or editing an existing graph, and a check box for including events from the History page. Life Form also gives you the option of viewing your data in either graph or report format with the Graph and Report radio buttons located in the lower left corner of the screen.

If you choose to view your data as a report, you will see something that looks like this:

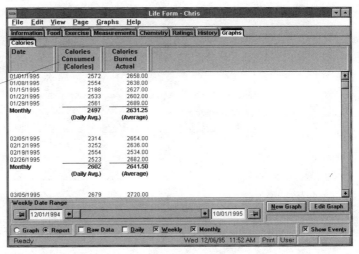

Data is displayed in columns in a report.

The Items list, date range, and controls are the same for a report as they are for a graph, except that the Raw Data, Daily, Weekly, and Monthly view options are represented by check boxes rather than radio buttons. Each report contains the following elements:

Title Row. Life Form displays headings for the items you include in your report along the top of the report in the title row.

Date Column. Dates for a report appear along the left side of the screen under the Date column heading.

Item Columns. Life Form displays data for the items you include in a report in columns. Each piece of data corresponds to a date listed in the Date column.

Deciding What to Graph

Before you create a graph, you will need to consider what items you want to include. You may want to compare items from the same page, such as *Calories from Fat*, *Calories from Carbohydrate*, and *Calories from Protein*. You might want to view items from different pages, for example, *Stress*, *Blood Pressure*, and *Aerobics:Calories Burned*. You can select up to six different items from the different pages. You should feel free to experiment and create a graph comparing anything and everything of interest to you. See the *Suggestions for Use* section of this chapter for examples of possible graphs you can create.

LIFE FORM TIP

Though a graph containing six items can look impressive, it can also be difficult to view and interpret. You might want to start by including only a few items on your graph and then experiment with adding more items as time goes by.

Creating a Graph

When you are ready to create a graph of your own, follow these steps:

✍ Or type Ctrl+I.

1. If a blank graph does not appear on the screen, click on the New Graph button. (You can also select New from the Graphs menu.) Life Form displays a new graph and highlights its tab.

2. With the tab highlighted, type a name for the graph not to exceed 40 characters. Then press Enter. If you do not enter a name, Life Form will continue to identify the graph by its default title, for example, *Graph A*.

3. From the list at the right of the program window, select up to six items to include in your graph.

✍You can include up to 6 items in a graph.

Click on the check box to the left of an item to select it. If you change your mind about an item, you can remove it from the graph by clicking again on its check box. Once you select an item, Life Form displays a number between 1 and 6 before its name. This number indicates how many items you have selected and the order they appear on the graph. If you try to select a seventh item, Life Form displays an error message.

Life Form automatically includes all items from all pages of the program in the list. If you know where an item is located, you can reduce the size of the list to find it more easily. If, for example, you know an item is found on the Ratings page, you can select Ratings from the Select Items By drop-down list (located directly above the Items list). When you do, Life Form displays only those items found on the Ratings page.

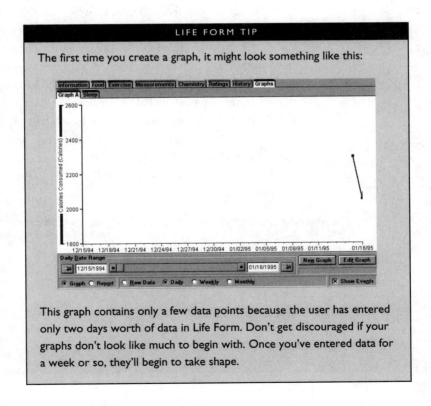

LIFE FORM TIP

The first time you create a graph, it might look something like this:

This graph contains only a few data points because the user has entered only two days worth of data in Life Form. Don't get discouraged if your graphs don't look like much to begin with. Once you've entered data for a week or so, they'll begin to take shape.

Creating a Report

When you create a graph, you also create a report. If you have already created a graph for a group of items and want to view the data in the form of a report, click on the Report radio button near the bottom left corner of the program window. If you haven't already created a graph for a group of items, you can create a report by clicking on the Report radio button and then following the steps described in *Creating a Graph*.

Using a Graph

Selecting a View for Your Graph

Life Form offers you five different views of the information you include in your graph. One is the report view, which you select by following the steps described in *Viewing a Report*. The remaining four views appear in graph format. The four different versions of a graph are *Raw Data, Daily, Weekly*, and *Monthly*. The Raw Data view shows all data entries, and can include more than one data point for each day. The Daily view displays one data point for each day with data. The Weekly view shows one data point for each week, and the Monthly view displays one point for each month. You can select a view for your graph by clicking on one of the Raw Data, Daily, Weekly, or Monthly radio buttons.

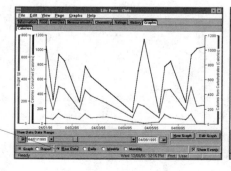

The Raw Data view can show more than one data point per day.

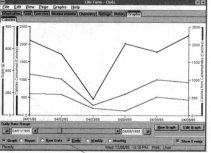

The Daily view shows one data point for each day.

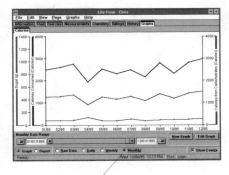

The Weekly view shows one data point for each week.

The Monthly view shows one data point for each month.

Note: To define what information is displayed on the Daily, Weekly, and Monthly views, see **Deciding How Data Points Are Calculated** *later in this chapter.*

Changing the Dates

Life Form automatically displays data for the last 30 days if you select the Raw Data or Daily view for a graph. The Weekly view spans the last 13 weeks or 1/4 year, while the Monthly view shows data for the past 12 months. If you want to change the beginning or ending date for a graph, type the new date in the appropriate box located at either end of the date range, and then press Tab. The new date will not take effect until you press Tab or click on another graph control.

Note: Any changes in date range you make to one view of a graph do not affect the other views of the graph, but they do affect the related report.

LIFE FORM TIP

You can move the graph ahead a day, a week, or a month at a time, depending on the view you have selected, by clicking on the right arrow at the right end of the date range scroll bar. You can move it back a day, a week, or a month by clicking on the left arrow at the left end of the date range scroll bar.

GRAPHS

Using the Push Pins

Each graph you create provides a window into the data you record using Life Form. As time goes by, your graphs move forward in time so the data you see is current. If you do not want a graph to keep moving, you can freeze it at either end using the push pins. If you click on the push pin at the left end of the date range window, the beginning date of your graph remains the same from day to day. The date range for the graph will continue to expand as time passes and more and more days are added to the right end of the graph. If you click on the push pin at the right end of the date range window, the ending date of your graph will be fixed. As time goes by, the date range of the graph will shrink as you approach the ending date. If you fix both ends of the graph with the push pins, you freeze the graph in time and it neither shrinks nor expands. Once you have pushed a push pin in by clicking on it, you can pull it out by clicking on it again. When you pull out a push pin, the previously fixed date remains the same until you use the scroll bar or change the dates, or until the date advances over time.

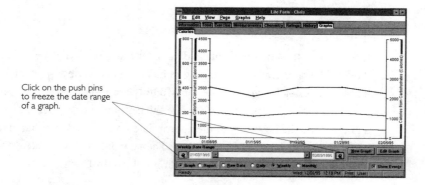

Click on the push pins to freeze the date range of a graph.

Showing Events

If you want to include events from the History on a graph, click on the Show Events radio button. When you choose this option, Life Form displays the events from the History page that you have marked for graphing as vertical lines on the graph. When you print the graph, basic information about each event appears below the graph.

Note: Only those events falling within the specified dates appear.

Events from the History page are displayed as vertical lines on a graph.

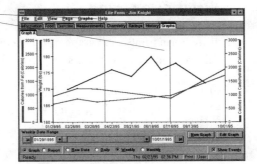

✎To view information about an event included in a graph, position the pointer over the event line and press and hold down the left mouse button.

Using the Reference Line

Because it may be difficult to determine the precise value of a data point just by looking at the graph, Life Form provides a tool called the reference line. The reference line is a horizontal line that you can move up and down the graph. As you move the line, Life Form displays values for a selected item in the Status bar. To use the reference line, position the pointer over the legend of the item whose data you want to pinpoint. Click and hold down the left mouse button so the reference line appears. Move the line up or down to view values for different data points or areas of the graph. If you position the pointer directly over a data point while still holding down the left mouse button, Life Form displays both the date and the value for the point.

The reference line appears when you click and hold down the left mouse button over an item's legend.

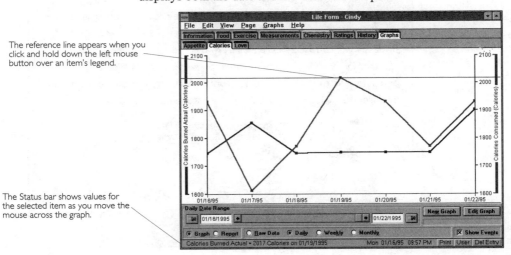

The Status bar shows values for the selected item as you move the mouse across the graph.

Printing a Graph

Life Form prints each graph *as it appears on the screen*. To print the active graph, follow these steps:

✎Or type Ctrl+P.

1. Click on the Print button in the Status bar. (You can also choose Print from the File menu.) The Print dialog box appears.

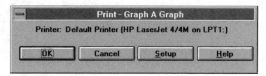

2. Select an orientation for your graph.

    You can print your graphs in either portrait or landscape orientation. All graphs are printed in landscape orientation unless you specify otherwise. If you want to print a graph in portrait orientation, click on the Setup button in the Print dialog box. Then click on the Portrait radio button, and press OK.

3. Choose OK. Life Form prints the graph.

LIFE FORM TIP

Life Form automatically prints graphs in landscape orientation to provide you a wider view of your data. If you prefer that Life Form print your graphs according to the current Print Setup selection, whether landscape or portrait, you can specify this as a preference. To change the graph print setting, choose Preferences from the File menu. Click on the *As Specified in Print Setup* radio button in the Graph Print Orientation group box, and select OK. If you change your mind later, you can return to the Preferences dialog and reselect the Landscape option.

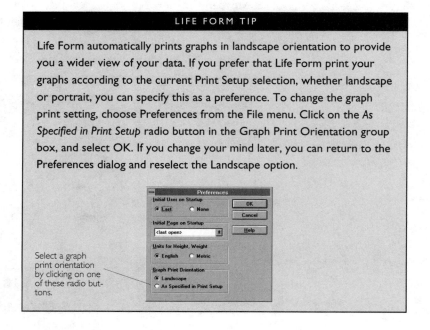

Select a graph print orientation by clicking on one of these radio buttons.

Using a Report

While graphs let you spot relationships between items visually, reports put the actual numbers in front of you. Viewing data for different items side by side can help you see exact values as well as weekly and monthly averages or totals. Reports can also be helpful for your doctor in making a diagnosis or monitoring your symptoms. If you prefer to view your data as a report, click on the Report radio button located in the lower left corner of the screen. Life Form displays dates along the left side of the screen and creates a data column for each item included in the report. If the report is wider than the program window, you can use the scroll bar at the bottom of the report to view the different columns.

Selecting a View or Views for Your Report

You can include raw, daily, weekly, or monthly values in a report, or any combination of the four by clicking on the Raw Data, Daily, Weekly, and Monthly check boxes. The dates included in the report are determined both by the smallest and largest view you select. Life Form begins with the range covered by the graph for the smallest view and extends it to meet the requirements of the largest view. If, for example, you choose the Daily and Weekly views, Life Form displays data for the range covered by the corresponding Daily graph. If the start or end date for the Daily graph falls anywhere but the beginning or end of a week respectively, Life Form extends the range so it begins on the first day of a week and ends on the last day of a week. By making these adjustments, Life Form can display accurate weekly values for the period covered by the Daily graph.

Raw Data. Raw data is displayed in a report according to the date it was entered.

Daily. If you select *Daily*, Life Form includes daily values in the report. If the Raw Data option has also been selected, the term *Daily* appears in the Date column and the daily value for each item in the corresponding row. The calculation method appears in parentheses under the daily value for each item. See *Deciding How Data Points are*

Calculated later in this chapter for more information on calculation methods.

Weekly. If you select *Weekly*, Life Form displays weekly values in the report. If you've also selected either the Raw Data or Daily view, the term *Weekly* appears in the date column after each seven days of data (based on a Sunday to Saturday week). Weekly values are displayed in the same row as this term, with the calculation method appearing in parentheses below each value.

Monthly. If you select *Monthly*, Life Form includes monthly values in the report. If you've selected any other view in addition to the Monthly view, the term *Monthly* appears in the date column under the last entry for the last day of each calendar month. Monthly values appear directly to the right of the term, with the calculation method appearing in parentheses below each value.

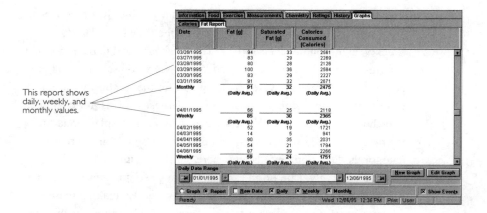

This report shows daily, weekly, and monthly values.

Changing Dates, Using the Push Pins, and Showing Events

You can change dates, use the push pins, and show events in a report using the same methods described in *Using Graphs*. If you include events in a report, Life Form inserts basic information about each event in the report.

Printing a Report

✍Or type Ctrl+P.

To print a report, click on the Print button in the Status bar, then choose OK in the Print dialog box. Life Form prints all the data in a report, regardless of what appears on the screen.

Editing a Graph

There are a number of things you might want to change about a graph once you have created it. You can pick different items to include in the graph, change their position in the graph, or edit the name of the graph.

Changing the Graph Name

✍Or select Edit Tab Name from the Graphs menu.

To change the name of a graph, double-click on the graph's tab, type the new name, and press Enter.

Changing the Items Included in a Graph

You can add, remove, and change items included in a graph by selecting and deselecting item check boxes. If the Items list is closed, click on the Edit Graph button to open it. If you have fewer than six items on a graph, you can add items to it. To *add* an item, click on its check box. To *remove* an item from a graph, deselect it by clicking on its check box. When you remove an item, Life Form renumbers the remaining selected items. To *change* the items included in a graph, add and delete them as described above.

Reordering Items on a Graph

Life Form places items in a graph in the order you select them. Once you have created a graph, you might want to change the position of the items you've included. The easy way to do this is to use the Show Checked Items feature. When you choose the Show Checked Items option from the Select Items By list box, Life Form reduces the list to only those items you have included in the graph. You can then reorder the items by clicking on their check boxes to deselect and reselect them in the desired order.

Hiding and Showing the Items List

You can hide the Items list to create more space for a graph on the screen. To hide the list, click on the Close List button. To re-open the list, click on the Edit Graph button or click on the Edit Graph option in the Graphs menu.

Resizing the Items List

You can change the size of the Items list by moving the left border to the left or right. To widen the list window, move the pointer over the left border of the list until the pointer turns into the resize symbol. Then press the left mouse button and hold it down as you drag the mouse to the left. To narrow the list, follow the same procedure but drag the mouse to the right.

Deleting a Graph

If you decide you no longer want a graph, you can delete it by following these steps:

1.   Click on the tab of the graph you want to delete.

✍*Or type Ctrl+D.*

2.   From the Graphs menu, select Delete Graph. Life Form displays a warning.

3.   Choose OK. Life Form deletes the graph.

Editing a Report

You can edit a report using the methods described in *Editing a Graph*. Any changes you make to the report appear in the corresponding graph when you select the graph view.

Advanced Features

This section covers advanced features of the Graphs page. Don't worry if you don't understand all the features described. While they can help you change your graphs to meet certain specifications, they are not necessary for using graphs on a basic level.

Editing the Way an Item is Displayed in a Graph

Once you have included an item in a graph, you can change the way it is displayed by editing its scale, units, or graph settings.

> ### LIFE FORM TIP
>
> Any changes you make to an item apply only to the *current view of the current graph*. Life Form does not record the changes to the item in its home page. If you want to change an item from the Ratings, Measurements, or Chemistry page so it will always be displayed the same way, edit its settings from the home page.

Changing the Scale

Life Form sets the vertical scale for each item in a graph based on the data you have recorded for that item. If you want to reduce or expand the range, you can set maximum and minimum values using the Scale group box. To change the scale, follow these steps:

✍Or double-click on the item's label.

1. Select the item you want to edit by clicking on its name in the Items list. (You can also choose Edit Item from the Graphs menu and make a selection from the list.)

2. Click on the Edit Item button. The Edit Item dialog box appears.

3. Click on the Set Limits Manually group box. Life Form displays the default values.

4. Edit the maximum and minimum values by typing your changes in the Maximum and Minimum text boxes.

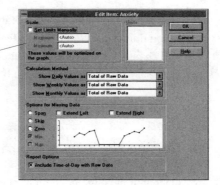

You can change the scale of a graph by entering new maximum and minimum values.

5. Choose OK. Life Form returns to the graph and adjusts the scale to meet your specifications.

Note: Life Form may still modify your manual limits slightly so they fit nicely on the graph.

Changing the Units

You can change the units for many different items, including duration and distance items from the Exercise page. You can also edit the units for Height and Weight and any duration items from the Ratings, Measurements, and Chemistry pages. To change the units for an item, follow these steps:

✎Or double-click on the item's label.

1. Select the item you want to edit by clicking on its name in the Items list. (You can also choose Edit Item from the Graphs menu and make a selection from the list.)

2. Click on the Edit Item button. The Edit Item dialog box appears.

3. Click on the Set Limits Manually group box. Life Form displays the default values.

4. Choose OK. Life Form displays the data using the new unit.

Deciding How Missing Data Is Graphed

There may be times that you leave holes in the data you enter using Life Form. You might take a vacation, get sick, or simply forget to enter data. In the case of exercise, you may not make any entries on the days you're inactive. Life Form considers gaps in data to be *missing data*. While missing data might not make a difference to you, it has an important effect on your graphs. The program can show missing data as a hole in your graph or display values for it in a number of ways.

Life Form gives you six options for graphing missing data: *Span, Skip, Zero, Mid, Min,* and *Max.* In addition to these options you can select *Extend Left* and *Extend Right* to plot data points for dates preceding or following the dates you've entered data. We've assigned the option or options that provide good results for each predefined item, so you don't have to worry about missing data if you don't want to. If, however, you define your own items or want to change the method we've assigned, you should be familiar with the different options.

Span. If you select the Span option, Life Form bridges gaps in data by drawing a straight line between the data points immediately preceding and following the gaps. *Span* works well for items that change gradually over time or are related to your body's shape and size, such as *Weight.* If you enter your weight only once a week, you want your graphs to show an approximation of your weight for the other six days. It is probably safe to assume that if you weighed 166 pounds last Monday and 164 pounds today, your weight dropped gradually over the course of the week. The same would apply for changes in other body measurements such as *Waist* and *Biceps.*

When you select *Span,* Life Form bridges gaps in data by drawing a line between data points.

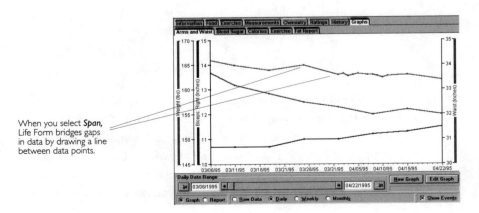

Skip. If you select the Skip option, Life Form leaves a blank space where there is no data. If, for example, you are tracking your calories and don't enter meals for one week, you will probably want Life Form to skip the week when plotting data points rather than making an estimate by spanning the data.

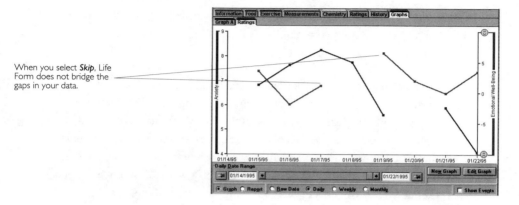

When you select *Skip*, Life Form does not bridge the gaps in your data.

Zero. Selecting the Zero option tells Life Form to display missing values as zero. This is the best option for exercise items. If you have not entered any exercise for a certain day, you probably want your graphs to show that you did not exercise by assigning a value of zero.

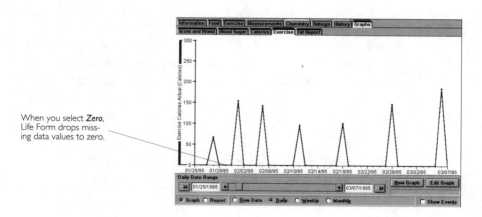

When you select *Zero*, Life Form drops missing data values to zero.

Mid. For those items with scales, you can choose the Mid option (referring to mid-point). When you select *Mid*, Life Form fills gaps in data with the middle scale value. If this sounds confusing, consider the example of *Fatigue*. If you measure *Fatigue* on a Lo to Hi scale, where Lo means completely exhausted and Hi means you are bursting with energy, the middle value represents how you feel on an average day.

By instructing Life Form to graph missing data as this middle value, you assume the condition was neither bad nor good, but average, during these times.

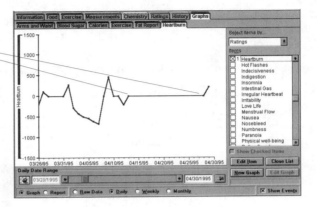

When you choose *Mid* for a scale item, Life Form assigns missing data the middle scale value.

Min and Max. The Min and Max options also apply to items measured on a scale. If you choose *Min*, Life Form plots missing data as the lowest value on the item scale. If you choose *Max*, it displays missing data as the highest value on the scale.

Extend Left and Extend Right. You can also extend your data to the limits of the graph by clicking on the Extend Left and Extend Right options. When you choose *Extend Left*, Life Form extends the line of data into the past. When you choose *Extend Right*, the program plots data into the future. These options are helpful with items that do not change over time, or for which you have not previously entered data. If, for example, your weight has remained relatively stable for the last few months, you can select *Extend Left*. This provides you with a view of your weight, so you can compare it to other items for which you have recorded data.

When you choose *Extend Left*, Life Form assigns the first value entered for an item to past dates.

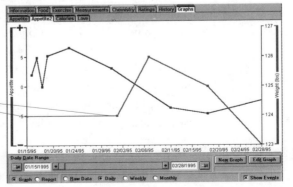

If you decide you want to change the options for missing data for an item, follow these steps:

✍ Or double-click on the item's label.

1. Select the item you want to edit by clicking on its name in the Items list. (You can also choose Edit Item from the Graphs menu and make a selection from the list.)

2. Click on the Edit Item button. The Edit Item dialog box appears.

3. Choose an option or options from the Options for Missing Data group box.

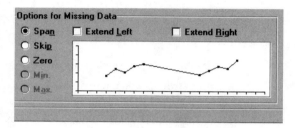

4. Choose OK. Life Form updates the graph according to your changes.

Deciding How Data Points Are Calculated

When you display a graph, you choose from four data options: *Raw Data, Daily, Weekly,* and *Monthly. Raw Data* represents the data you enter just as you enter it, or, in other words, no additional calculations are made that affect the data. The *Daily, Weekly,* and *Monthly* options can be displayed as averages, totals, minimums, or maximums of the values you enter for an item, or as the number of raw data points you enter for an item. *Weekly* and *Monthly* values can also appear as averages for days with data or averages of all days. These different options are called *calculation methods*. Life Form's predefined items have been assigned calculation methods to provide good graphing results. There may be times, however, when more than one method makes sense and you might want to view your data in different ways.

If you find calculation methods confusing, consider this example. Your doctor has told you that you need to reduce your blood glucose level, so you measure your blood sugar three times each day and record the results in the Blood Glucose item in the Chemistry page. There are many ways you can view your data in a graph to check your progress.

Raw Data. You can select the Raw Data view to see how your blood sugar fluctuates from morning to afternoon and from afternoon to night. Because no calculations are made when you choose *Raw Data*, you don't need to worry about calculation method. In this graph, you can tell that blood sugar consistently rises in the afternoon and drops at night.

The Raw Data view of this graph includes three data points for each day.

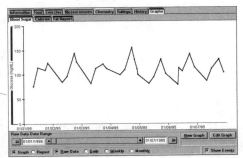

Daily Values. You might not want to clutter your graph with three data points for each day. When you choose the Daily view, Life Form calculates one data point for each day. There are five different possibilities for each point, which are determined by the calculation method you select. You can choose from *Average of Raw Data, Total of Raw Data, Maximum of Raw Data, Minimum of Raw Data,* and *Count.*

Average of Raw Data. If you select this option, the data point for each day is the average of the three values you enter, or the sum of the values divided by three. This calculation method is helpful if you want to get an idea of your general progress from day to day. The graph below shows that blood sugar both rose and fell over the course of the week.

Daily values in this graph are displayed as the average of all data entries for a day.

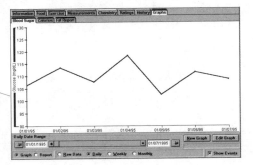

Total of Raw Data. If you select this option, the data point for each day is the total or sum of the three values you enter each day. You probably wouldn't use this option when tracking blood sugar, because totals would be difficult to interpret. This would be true especially if you measured your blood sugar a different number of times each day. Totals are helpful for viewing items such as *Calories Consumed* and *Calories Burned.*

The scale for the **Total of Raw Data** option includes a range of values much higher than the other options.

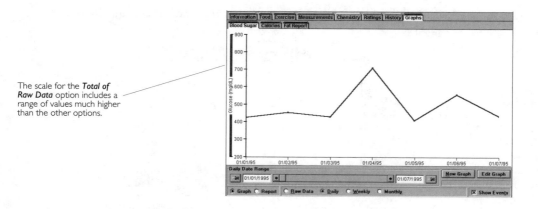

Minimum of Raw Data. If you select this option, the data point for each day is the minimum or lowest of the three values you enter. This method would be helpful if sudden drops in your blood sugar were a problem. By viewing the lowest value for each day, you and your doctor could try to determine how frequent or severe your problem is.

Minimum of Raw Data shows the lowest data point for each day.

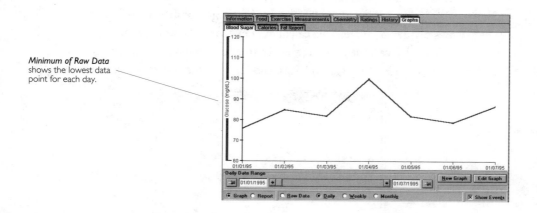

Maximum of Raw Data. If you select this option, the data point for each day is the maximum or highest of the three values you enter. This method would be especially helpful in determining periods when your blood sugar reached dangerous levels. It would also provide an alternative view of your general progress from the Average of Raw Data option.

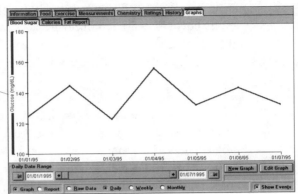

Maximum of Raw Data shows the highest data point for each day.

Count. If you select this option, the data point for each day is the number of entries made on that day. You could use Count to make sure you had entered your blood sugar three, and only three, times each day.

Weekly Values. If you have been recording your data for many weeks and want your graph to cover a greater range of dates than the daily graph, you might choose the Weekly view. With this view, Life Form calculates one data point for each week. When using the Weekly view, you can choose from the same five calculation methods provided by the daily view or select one of the two *Average of Daily Values* options. Choosing *Average, Total, Minimum, Maximum of Raw Data,* or *Count* provides the same general results as choosing the same option for daily values. In the case of monitoring your blood sugar, Life Form would make calculations using the 21 values you enter for the week rather than the three values you enter for the day.

Average of Daily Values (Days with Data). When you choose this option, Life Form calculates a daily average for the week based on the number of days you have entered data. For example, if you biked three days during the week for a total of 21 miles, the average of daily values (days with data) would be 7, or the total number of miles divided by the number of days for which data was entered. The daily values used in the calculation are either the average, total, maximum, minimum, or count of raw data, depending on which option is selected in the Show Daily Values As list box.

In the case of monitoring your blood glucose, the average of daily values (days with data) would give you alternate views for your averages, totals, maximums and minimums. If, for example, you selected Maximum of Raw Data for the daily calculation method and Average of Daily Values (Days with Data) for the weekly calculation method, the Weekly view would show you the average of your daily maximums for each week.

Average of Daily Values (All Days). If you select this option, Life Form calculates an average based on a 7-day week. In other words, the program divides the sum of daily values by 7, regardless of how many days you have entered data for the week. It is important to note that holes in data affect this calculation. Using the previous example, if you biked three days out of the week for a total of 21 miles, your average of daily values (all days) would be 3 miles, or the total number of miles biked, divided by the number of days in a week. If you wanted to view an average for only those days you biked, you would select the Average of Daily Values (Days with Data) method.

You could use the Average of Daily Values (All Days) method when monitoring your blood sugar, but the calculations would not be representative of your actual blood sugar level unless you entered data every day, without missing an entry. If you missed any entries, the resulting averages would be lower than your actual levels. This would happen because Life Form considers your blood sugar to be zero on days you do not enter blood sugar data.

Monthly Values. If you have been recording data for a long time, you might choose the Monthly view for your graph. The Monthly view shows one data point for each month. When deciding how you want your monthly data calculated, you have the same six options as you do for weekly data. If you choose the Average of Daily Values (All Days) option, Life Form divides the sum of daily values by the number of days in the month. For example, the September value on this graph is the sum of daily values divided by 30. The October value is the sum of daily values divided by 31. The same warnings that apply to the

Average of Daily Values (All Days) method when graphing weekly values apply to the method when graphing monthly values. Any holes in data will affect the calculations. For purposes of our blood glucose example, the various calculation methods provide the same basic results as described in the Daily and Weekly Values sections.

Monthly values are displayed as the average of daily values. Daily values are calculated as the total of raw data.

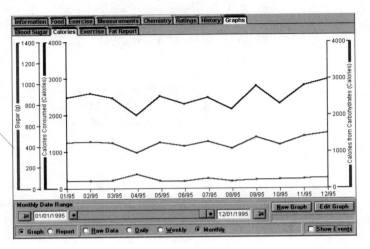

You can change calculation methods for an item from the Graphs page by following these steps:

Or double-click on the item's label.

1. Select the item you want to edit by clicking on its name in the Items list. (You can also choose Edit Item from the Graphs menu and make a selection from the list.)

2. Click on the Edit Item button. The Edit Item dialog box appears.

3. Select an option from each of the Daily, Weekly, and Monthly drop-down lists.

4. Choose OK. Life Form recalculates the data and updates the graph according to your changes.

Editing the Way an Item is Displayed in a Report

Any changes you make to an item in a graph also apply to the corresponding report. While the options for missing data are not relevant for a report, both units and calculation method are. If you are in a report, you can change the units or the way data is calculated for an item by following the steps described in *Editing the Way an Item is Displayed in a Graph*.

You can double-click on an item header to bring up the Edit Item dialog box.

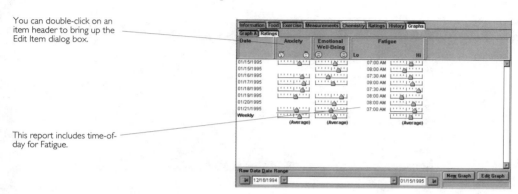

This report includes time-of-day for Fatigue.

In addition to these options, you have one other way to edit the way an item is displayed in a report. If you have included raw data in your report, Life Form displays the time-of-day for each piece of data. If you do not want the time-of-day to appear in your report, click on the Include Time-of-Day with Raw Data check box in the Edit Item dialog box to deselect this feature.

LIFE FORM TIP

If you include time-of-day for an item, Life Form creates a column to the left of the item's data column. This, in effect, doubles the size the item occupies on the screen. If you have included more than two items and choose the Include Time-of-Day with Raw Data option for each, you might not be able to see all the columns in your report on the screen. To view time-of-day in such a case, you can scroll across the report or print it.

Saving a Graph as a Graphics File

Life Form lets you save your graphs as bitmap files or Windows metafiles, so you can work with them as graphics outside of Life Form. To save a graph as a graphics file, make sure the graph appears on the screen and then follow these steps:

1. From the Graphs menu, choose Save Graph. The Save As dialog box appears.

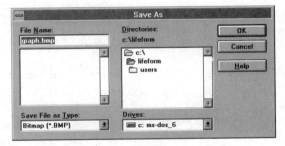

2. Enter a name for the file you are creating in the File Name text box.

3. Choose a type for the file from the Save as File Type list. You can choose from Bitmap (*.BMP) or Metafile (*.WMF).

4. If you want to save the file to a directory or drive other than the current one, choose the directory or drive.

5. Choose OK. Life Form saves the graph as a graphics file according to your specifications.

Saving a Report as a Text or Database File

Just as you can save your graphs as graphics files, you can save your reports as text or database files. This lets you work with your data outside of Life Form. To save a report as a text or database file, make sure the report appears on the screen and then follow these steps:

1. From the Graphs menu, choose Save Report. The Save As dialog box appears.

2. Enter a name for the file you are creating in the File Name text box.

3. Choose a type for the file from the Save as File Type list. You can choose from Text (*.TXT) or dBase (*.DBF).

4. If you want to save the file to a directory or drive other than the current one, choose the directory or drive.

5. Choose OK. Life Form saves the report as a text or database file according to your specifications.

Suggestions for Use

Using the Calories Graph

If you want to monitor the relationship between the number of calories you consume and the number of calories you burn, you can use the pre-defined Calories graph. To view the graph, click on the Calories tab.

Life Form will automatically plot points on the graph based on the information you enter in other parts of the program. Life Form calculates your calories burned based on your Weekly Lifestyle Activity from the Activity Level Setup and the exercises you enter on the Exercise page. It calculates your Calories Consumed based on the meals you enter on the Food page.

You can use the graph to help you monitor your progress toward weight loss, weight gain, or weight maintenance. If, for example, your calories consumed exceed your calories burned, you can expect to gain weight. If, on the other hand, your calories burned exceed your calories consumed, you can expect to lose weight. You will probably maintain your current weight if your calories burned and calories consumed are similar.

Differences between Calories Consumed and Calories Burned could account for weight gain or loss.

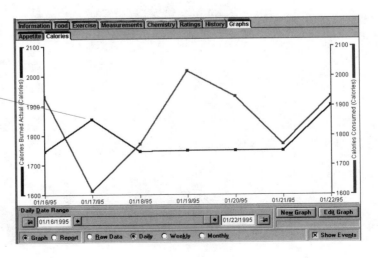

Using the Vitamins and Minerals Graph

Just as fats and carbohydrates are important to some, vitamin C and calcium are important to others. You can use the Vitamins and Minerals graph to track your intake of the vitamins and minerals included on the Nutrition Facts label. Life Form calculates the amounts of vitamin A, vitamin C, calcium, and iron you consume based on the foods you enter on the Food page. Values for these items are displayed as a percentage of the RDI, or Reference Daily Intake, as established by the FDA. To use the vitamins and minerals graph, click on the Vitamins tab.

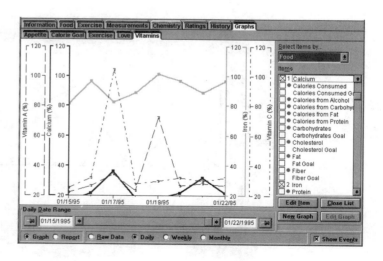

Using the Weight Graph

If you have set a goal for your weight on the Measurements page and are entering your actual weight on a regular basis, you can use the Weight graph to monitor your progress. The graph displays the Weight and Weight Goal items from the Measurements page. This graph is especially helpful if you've set a series of goals as milestones toward an eventual goal. If, for example, you wanted to lose 20 pounds in 5 months, you could use the graph to see if you are on track after the first week, first month, or any interval you choose.

Creating a Calorie Goal Graph

If you are trying to lose or gain weight, a Calorie Goal graph like this one can be helpful in monitoring your progress.

The Daily Calorie Goal you set on the Food page appears as a straight line on your Calorie Goal graph.

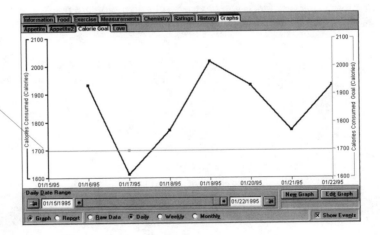

The graph compares the number of calories you consume to the daily calorie goal you set on the Food page. By examining the graph, you can easily tell whether you are under or over your goal. To create a Calorie Goal graph, you first need to set a Daily Calorie Goal on the Food page. To set your goal, follow these steps:

GRAPHS

1.   From the Food menu on the Food page, select Daily Nutrition Goals. The Daily Nutrition Goals dialog box appears.

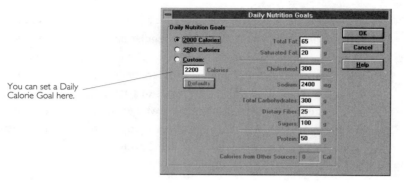

You can set a Daily Calorie Goal here.

2.   Click on the Custom radio button, and then press Tab.

3.   Enter your Daily Calorie Goal in the Calories text box.

4.   Choose OK.

Once you have set your goal, you are ready to create your graph. To create a Calorie Goal graph, follow these steps:

1.   From the Graphs page, click on the New Graph button if a blank graph does not already appear on the screen.

2.   Type a name for the graph in the graph tab.

3.   Click on the *Calories Consumed* and *Calories Consumed Goal* check boxes in the item list.

LIFE FORM TIP

Life Form treats the Calories Consumed Goal as a constant. In other words, it assumes that the goal applies to all dates in the past and future. This is why the goal is represented by a straight line on the Calorie Goal graph. If you change your calories goal, but want to view previous data against a previous goal, you should create a Calorie Goal item on the Measurements page. See *Creating a Goal Item* in the *Suggestions for Use* section of *Chapter 6, Measurements* for more information.

Creating an Exercise Graph

If exercise is important to you, you might want to create an Exercise graph to track your actual and estimated calories burned from exercise. Life Form calculates estimated values based on the number of exercise hours you enter in the Activity Level Setup. If you intend the estimate to be a goal, you can use the graph to track your progress. To create an Exercise graph, follow these steps:

1.   Click on the New Graph button if a blank graph does not already appear on the screen.

2.   Type a name for the graph in the graph tab.

3.   From the Select Items By drop-down list box, choose *Metabolism Estimate*. Life Form displays only the items used in calculating the Daily Metabolism Estimate.

4.   Click on the *Exercise Calories Actual* and *Exercise Calories Estimate* check boxes in the item list. Life Form plots the data for both items in the Exercise graph.

The Exercise graph below shows that actual calories burned from exercise exceed the estimate.

Your Exercise Calories Estimate appears as a straight line unless you've edited your Weekly Exercise Activity in the Activity Level Setup or changed your weight or height..

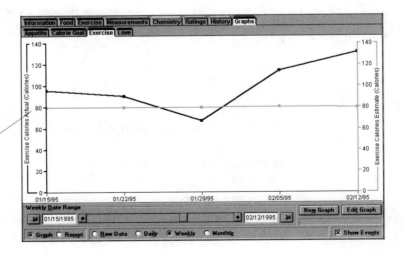

GRAPHS

Tracking a Special Diet with a Graph

Most diet programs require you to eat less of certain types of foods and more of others. Popular options include low-fat, high-fiber, low-protein, and low-carbohydrate diets. Life Form can help you track the different elements of your diet and chart your dieting progress. If, for example, your diet suggests you eat fewer than 30 grams of fat per day, you can see how close you come each day by graphing your fat intake (*Fat*) against the fat goal (*Fat Goal*) you set on the Food page. (*Note: For instructions on setting a Fat Goal, see* **Setting Daily Nutrition Goals** *in* **Chapter 3, Food**). You can add *Weight*, which you track on the Measurements page, to the graph to see how the change in your diet affects your weight.

If you consistently meet your dietary goals, but fail to lose weight, you might want to set a new goal, try a different diet, or look for other non-dietary factors that could be affecting your weight.

The following is a list of possible special diet graphs you can create.

Type of Diet	Items to Include
Low-Fat	Fat, Fat Goal
Low-Saturated Fat	Saturated Fat, Saturated Fat Goal
Low-Cholesterol	Cholesterol, Cholesterol Goal
Low-Carbohydrate	Total Carbohydrates, Carbohydrates Goal
High-Fiber	Fiber, Fiber Goal
Low-Sugar	Sugar, Sugar Goal

Tracking Training with a Graph

Graphs can be helpful if you train for a sport and want to monitor the effectiveness of your training. If, for example, you run marathons, you can create a training graph including items such as *Running:Dist./ Score, Running:Duration, Calories from Carbohydrates,* and *Sleep*.

Once you have completed your training and the race is over, you can add the race to your graph. To do this, enter the race as an event on the History page. Then click on the check box to the left of the event to indicate you want to include it in your graphs.

Once you have entered the race as an event, return to your training graph on the Graphs page. As long as the Show Events option is selected, Life Form includes the race in your graph. As you do this for all the races you run, you can evaluate the different factors in your training program based on your success in each race.

If you compete so often that you cannot easily view all your training periods in one graph, you might find it helpful to create a new graph for each training period. To do this, you can freeze the dates of the graph to match a training period by using the push pins at either end of the date range. Then name the graph after the race the training preceded. As time goes by and you compete more and more, you can compare the different training graphs.

Graphing Goals

If you're like most people, you set goals for yourself in an effort to improve your health. These goals can range from increasing fiber intake to cutting back on TV watching. You can use Life Form to set goals and track your progress in meeting them. There are two types of goal graphs you might want to create using Life Form. The first centers on a goal that remains constant, such as sleeping eight hours a day. The second targets a goal that changes over time, such as dropping from 25% body fat to 21% body fat by November 1. The following examples describe how to create Sleep and Body Fat Goal graphs. You can follow the examples to create these or other goal graphs.

Creating a Sleep Goal Graph

To create a Sleep Goal graph, you must first add a new item on the Ratings page. Name the item *Sleep Goal* and define it as a Date, Number type. Then select *Extend Left* and *Extend Right* in the Options for Missing Data group box in the Graph Settings window.

After you have set up the Sleep Goal item, enter the goal value in the first line. Then move to the Graphs page and create a new graph containing the Sleep Goal and Sleep items. Your goal appears as a straight line extending across the entire date range of your graph. If you have entered your actual sleep time from day to day, the data approaches and moves away from this line, depending on your progress

Your Sleep Goal appears as a straight line on the graph.

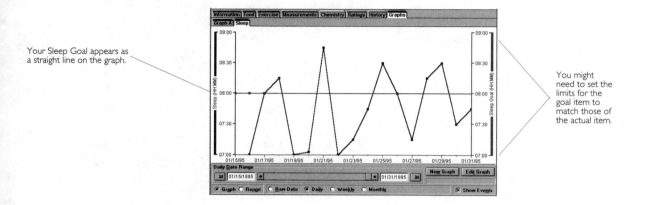

You might need to set the limits for the goal item to match those of the actual item.

Creating a Body Fat Goal Graph

To create a Body Fat graph, you will first need to create a Body Fat Goal item on the Measurements page. Name the item *Body Fat Goal* and define it as a Date, Number type. In the Body Fat Goal item, enter your actual body fat rather than your goal for the starting date. Then enter milestones along the way to the final goal, or just the final goal and date you want to reach it. The example below shows that you want to go from 25% to 21% over the course of eight months. You want to be 23% after four months.

When you create a graph including the goal item, Life Form spans the gaps between the data. The line the program draws between your original body fat and your goal body fat shows you what your progress should be over time. If you want to get an idea of how much body fat you should have lost by a certain date, you can use the reference line to view the value for that date.

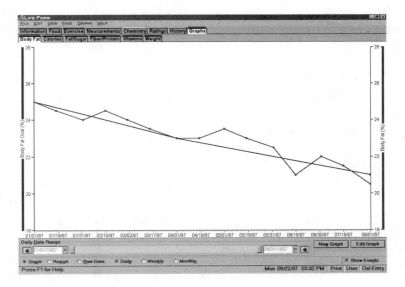

Creating a Growth Chart

If you have set your children up as Life Form users and want to monitor their growth, you can create a graph containing height and weight for each of them. The graph will reflect any changes you enter in the Height and Weight items on the Measurements page, and will resemble the growth charts kept by your pediatrician.

You can track your children's growth with a Growth Chart.

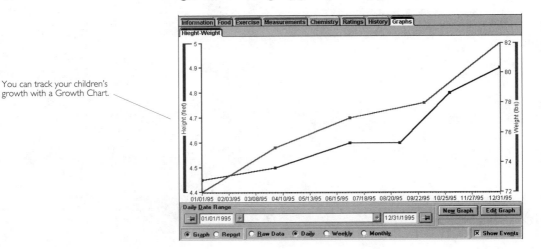

NOTES

Delays for Database Updates

There might be times when you open the Graphs page that Life Form displays this message: "Updating databases, please wait..." If you see this message, it means that you've edited some data on one or more of Life Form's other pages and the program has not yet finished updating the databases with the new information.

When you see this message, you have two options. The first is to wait for the program to finish the update. When it does, it will remove the message dialog from the screen. Your second option is to click on the Cancel button in the Life Form Update Status dialog box. If you do, Life Form displays this message: "Life Form will continue to update your databases in the background. Your graphs may not be accurate until Life Form finishes updating the databases."

You might never encounter the update messages when using Life Form.

INDEX

Database
    Methodology, 90-94
    Optimizing, *see Online Help
    System for details*
    Updates, 218
Dates
    Changing, 187, 192
    Entering, 114
Deleting
    an Exercise, 104
    an Exercise Record, 102
    an Event, 172
    a Food, 67-68
    a Graph, 194
    an Item, 151
    a Meal, 51
    a Record, 37, 146
    a User, 25
Density, 62, 64, 69-70, 77-79
Dentist Visit, 169-170, 174
Depression, 165
Deselecting Items, 15
Diarrhea, 165
Diet
    Low-Calorie, 82-83
    Low-Fat, 83-84, 214
    Low-Carbohydrate, 84, 137, 214
    High-Fiber, 84-85, 214
    Vegetarian, 85
Dizziness, 165
Doctor, 7, 33, 80, 83, 137, 157, 176-
    177, 191, 200, 202
Doctor Visit, 169-170
DOS, 3
Double-Clicking, 5
Dress Size, 132
DRV (Daily Reference Value), 89
Duration, 97-99, 109, 119, 147-148,
    159-160, 166, 196
Duration Properties, 109, 153

E

Earache, 165
Eating Habits, 9-10, 42, 75, 112, 115-
    116, 118
Editing
    Basic Information, 31
Editing
    an Event, 171
    an Exercise, 103-104
    an Exercise Record, 102
    a Food, 67, 79
    a Graph, 193-194
    Intensity,110-111
    an Item, 150-151, 195-205
    a Meal, 49
    a Recipe, 67
    a Record, 37, 146
    Tab Name, 193
    a User, 24
Emergency Phone Numbers, 31, 35
Emotional Well-Being, 165
Entering
    Basic Information, 31
    Data in Windows, 11-12
    Dates, 114
    a Doctor, 33
    an Emergency Phone Number, 35
    an Event, 169-170
    an Exercise Record, 98-99
    a Food in a Meal, 45-46
    Food Names, 46
    a Hospital, 34
    an Information Record, 32
    an Insurance Plan or Policy, 36
    a Meal, 44
    a Medical Condition, 34-35
    a Pharmacy, 36
    Quantities, 47
    Times, 115
Estimated Exercise Calories, 105-
    106, 120, 213